Empowering Vision

For Dreamers, Visionaries & Other Entrepreneurs

© 1986, 1987, 1988, 1991, 1992 by Marianne Weidlein

ALL RIGHTS RESERVED. No part of this book, other than worksheets clearly labeled "photocopy for your use," may be reproduced or transmitted in any form or by any electronic or mechanical means including information storage and retrieval systems without permission in writing from the publisher, except by a reviewer who may quote brief passages in a review. Published by Aimari Press, Boulder, Colorado.

Printed July 1992 - Second Edition
Printed July 1991 as *Empowering Vision — For Dreamers, Visionaries & Other Entrepreneurs*
(First printed as: *Visions & Business*)

ISBN 0-9629636-5-8

Library of Congress Catalog Card Number: 92-64232

Printed in the United States of America

Cover designed by Candyce Erwin, Marianne Weidlein, Jan Betts
Book design by Candyce Erwin and Marianne Weidlein
Artwork by Candyce Erwin

Quotes from *Accept This Gift* are reprinted with permission.

Aimari Press
P.O. Box 18296
Boulder, CO 80308-8296
(303) 442-0681

Acknowledgements

This manual would not have been possible without the initial catalyst of C. Srinivasan. Soon after, Cher Sider's encouragement spurred the first version, completed in January 1986. Kate Fotopoulos provided unconditional support, without which the first, and all succeeding versions, may never have been written.

Since then, the manual has been revised and edited many times, and with each revision new elements and new levels of understanding and sophistication have evolved. Although I formulated the concept and conceived the design of this multi-dimensional approach to "teaching" business, I needed a technician to help translate the material into a solid, comprehensive book. My request was answered by Stephanie Roth, without whom this manual would have remained only as handouts to a course.

Many others enriched this project with their contributions. I appreciate James MacRitchie, Jan Kristiarsson, Jessie Weber, Julia Lane, Mark Carson, Henry Aiy'm Fellman, Tim Marks, Gary Stokoe, Beverly Peterson, Barbara Ewing-Miner, Jan Betts, Rotha Randall, Tamara Chapman, Deborah Downs, Susan Fernie, Larry Paine, Joseph McCluskey, and Pardis Foroutan for their unique and essential support.

And of course, there is family. Thank you Krystie Seidel, Wayne Nelson, James Weidlein, Janet and Ken Hudonjorgensen, Patti and Hal Laipply for believing in me, and Candyce Erwin for the beauty and lightness you have given this book.

As with any process, *Empowering Vision for Dreamers, Visionaries & Other Entrepreneurs* belongs to all involved.

Table of Contents

List of Forms and Worksheets vii
Introduction viii
How to Use This Manual x

Section 1. Management

Introduction 1
Visioning 2
Life Purpose Visioning 4
    Activity 1. Life Purpose Vision 4
Current Visioning 7
    Activity 2. Current Vision 8
Evaluating Your Management Skills 10
    Activity 3. Self-Evaluation 10
Determining the Needs of Your Business 13
    Activity 4. Business Evaluation & Checklist 13
Organizing and Planning Your Business 19
    Activity 5. Organizing Your Business 20
Managing Your Time 24
    Activity 6. CPM Chart—Time Management Using the Critical Path Method 25
Your Typical Work Week 29
    Activity 7. Master Schedule 29
Planning Chart 32
    Activity 8. Planning Chart 32
Clarifying Your Service, Quality, & Professional Image 34
    Activity 9. Your Service, Quality, & Image 35
Choosing Your Income-Generating Program 37
    Activity 10. Narrowing Your Focus 37
Developing Your Income-Generating Program 39
    Activity 11. Program Planning & Development 39
Evaluating Your Workload 44
    Activity 12. Projecting Your Ideal Workload 45
Additional Management Materials 50
Fees, Discount, and Collections 50
    Activity 13. Fees, Discounts, & Collections 50
Making Agreements and Contracts 56
    Activity 14. Agreements & Contracts 57

Organizing Your Paperwork 59
    Activity 15. Filing System 59

Section 2. Marketing

Introduction 63
Market Research 63
An Overview of the Marketing Strategy 65
Targeting Your Clients 67
    Activity 16. Client Profile 67
Analyzing Your Competition 70
    Activity 17. Competition 71
Evaluating Your Service Industry 73
    Activity 18. Your Service Industry's Growth Stage 76
Positioning and Communication 80
    Activity 19. Positioning Objectives & Messages 81
Promotional Campaign Options 86
    Activity 20. Promotional Campaigns 86
        A. Advertising Campaign 87
        B. Direct Sales Campaign 92
        C. Sales Promotion Campaign 93
        D. Public Relations Campaign 95
Developing Your Promotion Plan 98
    Activity 21. Promotion Plan 99
Additional Marketing Information 102
Introduction to Sales 102
The Sales Process 103
Direct Sales Presentations 106
    Activity 22. Direct Sales - Phone Calls or Visits 107
How to Write A Cover Letter 109
    Activity 23. How to Write a Cover Letter 109
Developing Promotional Materials 111
    Activity 24. Planning Promotional Materials 112

Section 3. Financial Matters

Introduction 117
Basic Organizational Structures 119
Overview of an Accounting Strategy 120
Your Financial Map 122
Master Chart of Accounts 122
    Activity 25. Chart of Accounts 124
Budgeting 127
    Activity 26. The Budgeting Process 128

A Simple Bookkeeping System 133
    Activity 27. Receipts Journal 133
    Activity 28. Disbursements Journal 140
Financial Statements 145
The Profit and Loss Statement 145
    Activity 29. Profit & Loss Statement 145
Variance Statement 150
    Activity 30. Variance Statement 150
The Balance Sheet 155
    Activity 31. Balance Sheet 155
Taxes 159
Your Break-even Point 161
Fixed and Variable Expenses 161
    Activity 32. Break-even Calculation 162
Petty Cash Account 165
    Activity 33. Petty Cash 165
Reconciling Your Checkbook Balance 168
    Activity 34. Balancing Your Bank Statement 168

Appendices

Appendix A. *Glossary* 173
Appendix B. *Business Proposal* 181
Appendix C. *Resources for Starting a Business* 185
Bibliography 189
Index 191

List of Forms and Worksheets

Advertising Worksheet 91
Balance Sheet Worksheet 155
Bank Reconciliation Worksheet 171
Master Schedule Form 31
Petty Cash Record Form 167
Planning Chart 33
Profit and Loss Statement Worksheet 148
Promotional Materials Worksheet 112
Prospective Client Profile Form 105
Variance Statement Worksheet 153
Work Scheduling Worksheet 49

Introduction

Welcome to a journey! To provocative, enlightening, exciting change. Because you are reading this now, you are thinking about making a change in business. *Empowering Vision For Dreamers, Visionaries & Other Entrepreneurs* is written for a sole proprietor in a service business and is about changing your life. It is perfect for you now if you want to:

- Turn your dream into a successful service business
- Learn the basics of business
- Be clear, congruent, creative, and secure
- Feel empowered, with direction from your own plan
- Develop more strength, perseverance and integrity
- Experience mastery with business
- Help renew and balance our shared quality of life.

When you choose to be your own master and apprentice, as you create the changes you choose, and do well what you love, you better your life and the lives around you.

This happened for me when I began developing *Empowering Vision* in 1985, having just earned my degree in business, at the age of 41. My degree program taught me business theory and concepts but not the *process* of how to actually do business. It did little to help me know myself better, experience harmony with others, reach beyond limits, and be responsible and successful. I looked further for such courses, written and group, to no avail. Years of single-parenting and living on the edge told me that if I wanted more, I must create it myself.

So I began by asking myself a series of questions, beginning with, "what is business?" My answer was, "management, marketing and financial matters." Other questions followed naturally: "what is management? It's planning, organizing and administering a business, beginning with a vision, knowing my own business skills, knowing what the business requires, organizing all the details, and creating a timeline, and so forth." These are addressed in the first six activities in this course.

Each activity was developed in the same way, as I continued logically answering my own questions. Because I wanted to create a business design process that would serve others, as well, I then took those answers and turned them back into questions, structuring them into a decision-making/ design process. With help, first, from Kate Fotopoulos, then Stephanie Roth—a technical writer—*Empowering Vision* became a complete course manual.

Answering each of my own logically-sequenced questions, I empowered myself, created wonderful and lasting change, strength and trust, and a process to help others do the same. I've used, developed, edited and changed this process a dozen times, and it has been edited numerous times by others. I know it will be refined again.

In keeping with the discoveries I've made over years of exploration, this manual emphasizes both the human and technical factors of creating and refining a service business. The three sections—

which focus on management, marketing and financial matters—offer a progression of activities to help you explore and develop a different business function. Beginning with your vision, your dream or idea, use these activities to guide your business' formation, change or refinement. Use them from the beginning, as a process of development, or use them individually as you see fit.

Empowering Vision will help you create your reality from your dreams. Not only will you learn about starting and nurturing a business, you'll learn to address sabotaging resistance, fear and limitation. This is a design process, a tool for self-reflection, empowerment, success and self-mastery. Some questions may be inappropriate for your needs. Use your discretion. Others may seem repetitive, yet are valuable because they explore variations of issues that will surface as you develop and operate your business. Just read, follow the steps, use your discretion to do what's right for you, and your life will be as you want. You'll make a contribution and feel more solid and secure in the process.

You will find this course refreshingly simple to use. You will move, carefully, one at a time, through steps you choose to take, from planting the seed to the harvest (including the bookkeeping for your harvest!). As you release resistance and fear, you will be empowered by what you know and are ready to do—now and in the future—for both your vision and the service of others. Go at your own pace, revisioning and redesigning whenever you need.

In the six years I've used this process with hundreds of people, I've seen miracles: people who double their income in only a month. I've seen others resist, run and dig even further into patterns of resistance, denial and over-extension. And I've seen everything in between. Anything is possible. I, too, have experienced extremes, all of which is natural and to be expected in the process of mastery.

Empowering Vision For Dreamers, Visionaries & Other Entrepreneurs is not just a tool and course. It is a way of thinking and being. How to use it is your freedom of choice.

Feedback and suggestions have been valuable for on-going development and refinement. Share your ideas and comments by writing me in care of the publisher.

Follow your heart and enjoy your journey!

Marianne Weidlein
May 1991

How to Use This Manual

This process is intended to draw from you exactly what you want—through your business—and to assist you in acknowledging and releasing the self-limiting patterns that inhibit your success. Sometimes, coming face to face with limiting patterns, and even your passions and dreams, may cause you discomfort. This is natural. It indicates that the process is working.

If you experience resistance or fear, ask yourself why, then determine what you will do about it, using the self-reflective questions at the end of each activity. Or you may want to set the course aside for a few days and do something different. Welcome your feelings and this opportunity to know yourself better. You can change the quality of your life, as well as build character, skill and strength. Use it well.

Choosing life circumstances based on true self-knowledge, you experience the sheer delight of successful self-employment. Self-awareness—awareness of your thoughts and feelings and all they express—is the first essential step toward overcoming inhibiting limitations.

Begin by reading through the manual, listing the activities you need, then work through them and any others of your own choosing. As you gain new insights, you will experience changes in your attitude and in your relationship with yourself and others. To keep current with your changes and new ideas, reuse the appropriate activities. As you continue this exploration, you and your business will continue to grow and develop. Once you have experienced this process, you will know which activities to use to make further changes.

Each of the three sections in this manual begins with a general concept and ends with specific conclusions. Where appropriate, a structure, such as a budget, time plan, promotion plan or bookkeeping system, is provided.

Using this question-asking process is empowering, for you draw on your own ideas, inner knowledge and willingness. What is right for you may not be right for someone else. As you develop your ideas into your own business, you are empowered...seeing yourself more clearly, learning and developing business skills.

Even if you delegate responsibility for the management of your business, success requires that you understand business and make decisions that result in the consequences you want. The bottom line is to gain the greatest exposure to your potential client and use your resources wisely. You are investing in yourself, your dreams and the quality of your life.

Following are suggestions to consider before you begin this life-changing adventure. Consider these carefully, for if you want to be successful, you need to know yourself, you need to stand on honest, empowering principles and to do everything with respect and commitment.

1. **Create an Agreement with Yourself.** Begin by developing your business from true and basic values and principles. Integrity is the key to success and peace of mind.

- Create a statement of policies to give to clients to read and sign. Live up to those policies.

- Be on time for all business appointments. If you foresee that you will be late, let the other(s) know as soon as possible.

- Make telephone calls and write letters when you say you will. Maintain honest and caring relationships with the people important to your success. Do what you say.

- Complete all projects on time. If you know you will be delayed, let the other(s) involved know as soon as possible. If you change your mind, let others know immediately.

- Respond to all referrals within seven days. This will keep your business alive and growing.

- Communicate. Express relevant thoughts, ideas, feelings and concerns.

- Add your own agreements:

-

-

Copy this Agreement onto your letterhead, sign it, and ask the person you think most believes in you to be your witness. Use this agreement with those who are key to the success of your business, especially those with whom you have contractual arrangements. Some people may feel uncomfortable with this commitment. If so, take the opportunity to discuss their misgivings, decide how you both want to respond, and watch what happens.

2. **Mentors.** Another way to empower yourself is to create a relationship with several successful people who agree to be mentors. These should be people who are strong and expert in your areas of focus; caring people who want to see you succeed. Seek support with the design and management of your business. Use your Agreement together.

3. **Scheduling.** Because Empowering Vision is a design process, you can maximize results by setting aside periods of time—one to three hours each—to use it. To realize the full value of this process, complete each activity before going on to another.

4. **Before you begin answering the questions, read each activity.** Evaluate it, then determine the level of detail you currently need. Not all questions will apply to your business, so answer only those that do, using complete thoughts and sentences. Organize your answers in a binder, folder or computer.

5. A **Glossary** is included in the Appendix to define terms you may not be familiar with. You may read about new concepts and definitions that differ from those you are used to. Be open. Just consider them, and if they fit your perception, use them. If not, just go on.

6. **Be neat.** Your plans are living documents. Use pencil and a good eraser or word processor so you can make changes easily.

7. **Worksheets.** After you've read through the manual, make copies of the worksheets you want to use. Keep the originals clean for future copying.

8. **Self-reflection.** Be willing to look at yourself, be more open and honest. If you experience fear, resistance and limitation, or just feel stuck, evaluate the issue from every perspective. Determine the source of the issue and resolve it before you move on. If you are experiencing these as you complete an activity, you will surely experience this when you do your business. As you drop self-imposed limitations, you empower yourself, the key to success with this process.

9. **Future planning.** Many of the activities in this manual will be useful in future planning sessions. After you complete the entire process, use selected activities independently to think through a new idea, plan a new program, redesign a current one, or create a new system or strategy. The activities are great if you just want to stir things up and see what happens!

Above all, remember that business is fun, exciting and just about the best way to become secure and confident. If you think your plan through carefully and stand behind your choices, you can do as you choose, so long as you respect the law and social demands. Know that what's important is to figure out what you want—what is true for you—and then create it.

◆

Whatever you vividly imagine, ardently desire, sincerely believe, and enthusiastically act upon ... must inevitably come to pass.

Paul J. Meyer
Success Motivation Institute

Management

Introduction

Business management is the process of visioning, goal setting, planning, organizing, and controlling your actions, resources, and personnel in order to realize your life's purpose and give form to your dream. Self-management is the process of becoming clear about what you really want, then identifying and releasing self-limiting patterns. Self-management will allow you to trust yourself and will free your creative strength. In the process, you will become more open and eager to learn. These are the prerequisites for success.

The activities in Section 1 will give you the skills necessary to design and manage your service as a strong, successful business. These include visioning, goal setting, organization, planning, time management, and administration. They all contribute to and form the foundation for an effective promotion plan and careful financial management.

Visioning and goal setting provide the foundation from which all further business decisions and actions evolve. The activities in the Management section will help you evaluate your service from philosophical, planning, administrative, and organizational perspectives. You will begin by visualizing the peak of your success, then evaluating your present circumstances, describing your preferred lifestyle, and finally outlining the steps you will take to make it a reality.

To allow your vision to become real also requires that you recognize and release self-limiting patterns. The visioning activities will help you evaluate your limiting patterns, identify and release your fears, recognize and accept your real limits, gain the knowledge you need, and thus make informed, solid decisions.

> *"Without this playing with fantasy, no creative work has ever yet come to birth. The debt we owe to the play of the imagination is incalculable."*
> Carl Gustav Jung

Visioning

Many of us have a dream, a vision, a deep yearning for a different lifestyle. Yet, we yearn for this vision in the privacy of our minds. Though we experience dissatisfaction, frustration, resentment, and even anger, we resist making change. (That's true even for those of us who earn our livings helping others to change.) Through this debilitating pattern, we squander strength, creativity, and intelligence. We end up coping with what we don't want, rather than developing positive attitudes, beliefs, and daily patterns.

> *"Dreams show you that you have the power
> to make a world as you would have it be."*
> Accept This Gift

Our dreams and visions creatively present to our active, conscious mind our unfulfilled needs ("I want security") and desires ("I want a comfortable lifestyle"). Once we translate these yearnings into a concrete picture or vision, once we begin identifying changes, making decisions, and taking action, we draw our yearnings into our everyday life.

A vision contains the power to facilitate substantial change in the quality of life. Satisfying our needs and desires is essential to our basic security, happiness, and success. Certainly, just using our intelligence to transform our limitations into self-honoring actions is a major contribution in itself. The resulting peace of mind leads to success and increased joy in living. As more of us live in this creative state, our world will thrive. This gift is for ourselves, for each other, and for future generations.

The visioning activities that follow will help you to draw your unfulfilled needs and desires to your conscious awareness. These activities will help you clearly visualize how you want to integrate your dreams and desires into your everyday life. By writing out the details, you will begin to experience your dream. As you experience it, you will begin to feel comfortable with it. Secure in your ability to create it, you will begin believing in it. Then, when you remember your vision, you will strengthen it. It, in turn, takes on a life of its own and begins to empower you.

The rewards of visioning are multidimensional: they include self-awareness, self-management, enhanced skill level, and, of course, empowerment—all indispensable components of success. Self-awareness helps you identify and address your limitations. Self-management frees you from limitations and allows you to weave your vision into the fabric of your everyday life. Skill development speaks for itself. And empowerment sets you free to do it all.

The visioning process also involves supporting yourself through use of resources: time, energy, money, things, and people. You are surrounded with all the resources you need to create what you want. To make major change, you need support; therefore, identify your real supporters.

The visioning activities that follow will help you clarify what you think is the purpose of your life, the life function that practically actualizes it, and the career and lifestyle that will fulfill these. An essential component of visioning is identifying the fears, resistance, and self-limiting patterns that inhibit the decision-making that allows your unique creativity to flow. Vision whenever you need to make major life changes or decide on smaller issues.

The complete visioning process involves two steps:

- Complete Activity 1, Life Purpose Vision, to clarify your purpose, function, and vision, and to identify limitations and establish goals.

- Complete Activity 2, Current Vision. This will help you identify immediate changes and goals, and determine the time frame within which you will realize them.

When you begin directing yourself toward what you really want, you will notice that many small changes begin producing major changes. Your success, happiness, and fulfillment will clearly reflect your new approach.

Note: Whenever you vision, it is ideal to go to a quiet place where you will be uninterrupted for several hours. If you are not sure that you will be undisturbed, save the activity for another time. Complete each question fully before you do the next. If you are interrupted, be sure to refamiliarize yourself with your answers when you return to the activity.

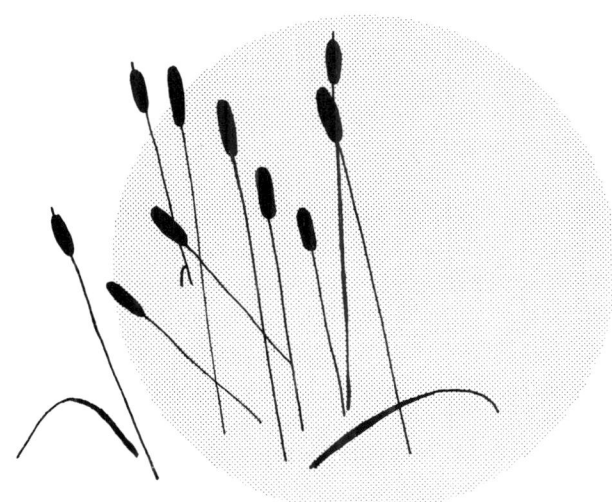

Empowering Vision

Life Purpose Visioning

When self-employed, you learn quickly that your actions shape the quality of your life. Your ability to thrive is in your hands, and your lifestyle is the result of the money you generate. Clarify your purpose, function, and vision, offer your service to those who are ready to buy, and you will succeed.

The Empowering Vision philosophy says that you have the right, the power, and the resources to create what you want just by being clear and releasing fear, self-limiting attitudes and patterns. Allow yourself to visualize your dream, uncensored by the restrictions and conditioning from your past.

You might find it helpful to ask someone to read you the following questions. Or you might want to tape record the session, or ask a friend to write down your important thoughts, in your words, as you respond to the questions. If needed, ask your friend to help draw out your vision by asking additional probing questions based on your responses.

Complete Activity 1 any time you want to:

- Focus your goals over a long period of time
- Clarify your purpose, function, or vision
- Review your long-term goals.

✍ Activity 1. Life Purpose Vision

Visioning For Earth: Begin by positioning yourself in a comfortable sitting or reclining position. Close your eyes if someone is reading the instructions. Close them between instructions if you are reading them to yourself. Read the following slowly, giving yourself ample time for complete responses.

Focus your attention on your breathing. Take several slow, deep, releasing breaths. As you release each breath, let all thoughts go with it. Continue this slow, deep breathing as you place yourself ten years from now on a beach next to a stream flowing out to sea. Look around you, and describe to yourself what you see.

As you look carefully at the scene you have just created, visualize the quality of life you want for the sky and air, for the birds, the trees and vegetation. Visualize the quality of life you want for the sand, soil, and the insects. Look again at the stream and visualize the quality of life you want for the fish and plants in the stream, and watch the stream flow into the ocean and meet the tide. Now, visualize the quality of life in the ocean—its vegetation and minerals, the fish and water animals. Explain to yourself why this quality of life is important to you.

And now, as you continue to visualize yourself sitting on the beach, envision people on the beach the way you want them to be together. Describe what they are doing. Imagine what they are saying to each other. Listen to the music in their voices. Describe the feeling of what you hear. Notice what you are feeling now, as you envision these people talking and sharing together. Experience this feeling flowing throughout your body as you continue to breathe, slowly and deeply.

And now determine how this visualization has been valuable for you. When finished, return to the present and open your eyes. Explain what you gave yourself through this visualization.

> **"Is our collective intelligence
> the brain of Gaia (the Earth)?
> What is the proper function of humankind
> within the evolving consciousness of the larger organism?"**
> Danaan Parry

With this visualization completed, answer the following questions.

1. **Purpose.** What do you think is the fundamental purpose of your life? If you are not sure, what is your best guess? Your purpose should reflect the reason you believe you are alive for yourself, not for others.

2. **Function.** Based on this purpose, what do you think is your function in society? How will your function help the planet reach the quality of life you envisioned above?

3. **Peak of Success Vision.** In the same reflective mood, consider the point in your life at which you sense you will be at the peak of your success. When do you think that will be? If you don't know, guess. Begin by writing the year and your age. Now, consider the quality of life you want for yourself at that time.

   Note: Answer in complete sentences. Visualize how you want to be living and experience how you want to feel. As you do, you will begin to feel this way.

   Describe:
   • Where you want to live
   • Your home environment and the people you live with
   • Service, career and business
   • Financial matters
   • Professional support network
   • Family, friendships and other relationships
   • Spare time
   • Your personal needs, health and well-being
   • Spirituality
   • Your modes of creative self-expression
   • How you are empowered.

   Above everything else, what do you want for yourself in your life?

When you have finished your vision, using a copy of the planning chart on Page 33, write the titles of each category above in the spaces provided. Identify key elements of your vision, then write them in abbreviated terms in the appropriate category.

4. **Support:** How do you believe you are supported to fulfill your purpose, function, and vision? When you want support, where do you seek it? When you don't feel supported, what do you do? Determine the effectiveness of this strategy. How do you want to feel supported? What will you do to experience the support you want?

5. **Limitations:** List and describe the self-limiting beliefs, fears, and patterns, by which you currently feel inhibited. Example: "I fear rejection, so I don't reach out." How does this affect you? Identify what you are ready to change and explain how you will accomplish it. With what will you replace these limitations?

6. **Shadow:** What need, desire or aspect of personality, do you most suppress or fear? For example, do you fear your anger? Or perhaps you suppress positive feelings, such as sensitivity, or your desire for intimacy or success. (If you are not sure, ask someone close to you.) Why do you suppress or fear this? Explain how suppressing this affects you. Determine how you will stop suppressing this, and how you will allow yourself more freedom of expression. Describe how you will feel as you experience freedom from supressing this. Describe how your purpose, function, and vision will be enhanced.

7. **Resources:** List your internal strengths and resources and explain how they empower you. List needed external resources and explain how you will utilize them to create change. Include dates when appropriate.

8. **Conclusion:** How do you feel now? Why? Describe what you have gained from this visioning. Write a commitment statement to yourself and to your purpose, function, and vision. Share it with your mentors and the people closest to you, so that they are better able to support you.

◆

"Until one is committed there is hesitancy, the chance to draw back, always ineffectiveness. Concerning all acts of initiative (and creation), there is one elementary truth, the ignorance of which kills countless ideas and splendid plans: that the moment one definitely commits oneself, then providence moves too.

All sorts of things occur to help one that would never otherwise have occurred. A whole stream of events issue from the decision, raising in one's favor all manner of unforeseen incidents and meetings and material assistance, which no man could have dreamt would have come his way."

W.H. Murray

Section 1. Management

Current Visioning

Look at your life as it is now. What is going on? Why? How do you feel about the way your life is? What do you want to change? How will you accomplish this? These are all essential questions. Once you answer them, commit to the decisions and steps that will make desired changes. Self-empowered, you can do everything you yearn for in the way and at the time of your choice.

Now that you have completed your Life Purpose Visioning, and are clear about your direction, complete Activity 2, Current Vision. In this activity, you will determine the objectives and changes that will make your vision a reality. Your Current Vision is the foundation of this course All business planning and promotional goals develop from the way your life is now, the way you want it to be, and the decisions that will facilitate change.

*"Listen silently and learn the truth
of what you really want.
No more than this will you
be asked to learn."*
Accept This Gift

Empowering Vision

✍ Activity 2. Current Vision

1. **Current Vision.** How do you want your life to be now? Describe:

   Note: When you are finished with your vision, using a copy of the Planning Chart on Page 33, write the titles of each category above the space provided. Identify key elements of your vision, then write them in abbreviated terms, in the appropriate category.

   - Where you live
   - Your home environment and the people with whom you live
   - Career and business
   - Financial matters
   - Professional support network
   - Family, friendships and other relationships
   - Spare time
   - Your personal needs, health and well-being
   - Spirituality
   - Your modes of creative self-expression
   - How you are empowered.

2. **Objective.** What is your current major objective?

3. **Change Goals.** List and describe the changes you are ready to begin making. Be realistic and honest with yourself about the immediate changes you are ready to make. Arrange these according to priority, beginning with the most important. Include dates when appropriate.

   > *"The first change is that your dreams of fear
   > are changed to happy dreams."*
   > Accept This Gift

4. **Completion Goals.** List and describe those incomplete or unresolved past goals, including—ideas, projects and relationships—that you are now prepared to complete. Review these and arrange them in order of priority. Include dates when appropriate.

5. **New Project Goals.** List and describe the new ideas and projects, not included above, that will enable you to create your vision. Include back burner projects that you have been thinking about and are ready to do. Arrange in priority order; include dates when appropriate.

6. **Limitations.** Describe your self-limiting beliefs, fears, and patterns. What are you ready to change? Explain how you will accomplish this. What will you replace these with?

7. **Shadow.** What need, desire, or aspect of personality do you most suppress or fear? This can be negative or positive (see Activity 1, Question 6). If you are not sure, ask someone close to you. Why do you suppress or fear this? Explain how suppressing this affects you. Determine how are you will stop suppressing this and how you will allow yourself more freedom of expres-

sion. Describe how you will feel as you experience freedom from suppressing this. Describe how your life will be enhanced.

8. **Resources.** List your strengths and internal resources and explain how they empower you. List needed external resources and explain how you will utilize them to create change. Include dates when appropriate.

9. **Conclusion.** How do you feel now? Why? Describe what you have gained from doing this visioning process. Write a commitment statement to yourself and your vision. Share this with your mentors and the people closest to you, so that they are better able to support you.

10. **Self-empowerment.** Reflect on your experiences while completing this activity and describe the ways in which you feel empowered.

Note: Go through your appointment book, review your schedule for the next several months, and evaluate your personal and professional commitments for this period. What appointments, workshops, classes, special events, holidays, vacations, business trips, and visits from out-of-town guests are listed? Determine whether they support you. Do you still want to do them? If not, how will you respond? If you remember any commitments you have not written in your book, add them now. Then add the activities you have set as goals.

A Reminder: Re-visioning every six months or so will help expand your previous vision. It will help you to revise goals as you and your circumstances change. If you are clear about what you want, if you are willing to acknowledge your self-limiting patterns and take steps to release them, you are empowered. As you consider new ideas, projects, and relationships, ask yourself: Will this:

- Fulfill my purpose, function and vision
- Help finish incomplete projects
- Actualize current goals, activities and projects
- Help release self-limiting patterns
- Adequately utilize my inner and outer resources
- Empower me?

Do I want to do it?

◆

*"The power of our consciousness
is such that just by holding that vision,
by affirming the possibility of it,
we begin to behave differently.
Actions begin to take place
that create the realization of that vision.
That's a far greater power than we ordinarily recognize."*
Willis Harmon

Empowering Vision

Evaluating Your Management Skills

When self-employed, you are both the business and the business manager. The quality of your service, the reputation of your business, your income and lifestyle all extend from the way you are—from your attitudes, behavior, and relationships, as well as from your skill level and expertise.

As the sole proprietor of a service business, you are responsible for planning, daily administration, marketing, and accounting. When you neglect any of these or the small, seemingly insignificant activities within any of these functions, your success and income are necessarily affected.

Activity 3, Self-Evaluation, helps you evaluate your skill level within the context of your vision and income needs. Recall your vision, then honestly evaluate the attitudes and behavior, abilities and skills that affect your business success. This self-evaluation will help you make decisions to increase your effectiveness as a manager. This, in turn, will enable you to create the lifestyle you want.

> *"Any manager's job is to take control of the resources available and to use them efficiently. The first and most important of those resources is his own time and talent."*
> Peter F. Drucker

Activity 3. Self-Evaluation

1. Why do you choose self-employment? Determine whether your choice is primarily a resistance to working for others or a readiness to express your unique creativity and create your own success. Explain fully.

2. Why do you choose this service business? Which of your personal needs and desires does this business satisfy?

3. On a scale of 1-10 (with ten being the highest), rate your confidence in your prospects for success. Explain your rating. What will increase it? Describe your patterns with setting goals, staying focused, and being organized. Consider your:

    - Commitment to yourself
    - Ability to take responsibility for your decisions and actions
    - Motivation, discipline, and perseverance
    - Ability to stay connected in relationship
    - Confidence with decision-making
    - Responses to disappointments and to the unexpected
    - Ability to be on time.

4. Does your business excite you? Why? Describe what would make you even more excited.

Section 1. Management

5. Describe how you want your management and marketing functions to be handled at the peak of your success. Will you perform these functions yourself, or will you hire or contract someone to manage and market your service?

6. On a scale of 1-10 (with ten the highest again), rate the general quality of your service. Explain. What are its strengths? What are its limitations? How do you feel about your rating?

7. Describe the kind of business manager you want to be. What will raise your managerial performance to that level? How will you accomplish this? What more will you ask from yourself to do so? Explain what kind of help you will need from your mentors, resources, and clients.

> *"You've got to come up with a plan.*
> *You can't wish things will get better."*
> John F. Welch

8. In your own words, define the following functions in your business:

    • **Management**   • **Planning**   • **Marketing**   • **Accounting**

    Compare your responses to the definitions in the Glossary.

9. Using the following Rating Chart, rate your interest level, as well as your current and preferred skill levels. Evaluate each rating, reflect on why you chose it, and explore how you feel about it. Add your scores and divide by four to obtain your overall rating as a business manager. Determine how your overall rating affects the success you envisioned in Activity 1, Life Purpose Vision. In the right hand column write your learning and skill development goals.

INTEREST LEVEL AND BUSINESS SKILLS RATING CHART				
	Interest Level	Current Skill	Preferred Skill	Learning & Skill Development Goals
Management				
Planning				
Marketing				
Accounting				
TOTALS				
DIVIDE BY 4:				

10. List and describe the possible circumstances and changes that could limit your business in the next few years. (These circumstances might include the economy, general trends in your industry, laws governing your business, your personal life, health, family, and so forth.) Now describe how you will address these if they occur. Discuss them with your mentors and your support system, as appropriate.

11. Do you want to enhance your credibility by the way you project yourself and interact with others? Explain.

12. Recall and describe the fears, resistances, or self-limiting patterns you experienced while answering these questions. What self-limiting patterns are you ready to release in order to strengthen your business skills? List them according to priority and explain what you are ready to do about them. Are there any patterns that you resist addressing? Explain.

13. Reflect on the important points this activity revealed, and describe the ways in which you feel empowered.

14. What must you learn and develop to be a more effective business manager? What resources are you ready to draw upon? Describe what you want from your mentors and support network. List the steps you will take and include dates when appropriate.

Note: You might want to repeat this self-evaluation after completing the activities in this manual, and, perhaps, after each time you re-vision. With practice, you will become a better manager than you ever expected!

◆

*"Every person, and all the events of your life,
are there because you have drawn them there.
What you choose to do with them is up to you."*
Richard Bach

Section 1. Management

Determining the Needs of Your Business

If you are just beginning your service business, your decision to use this manual shows that you recognize the need to build a solid foundation for your business. Similarly, if you have been in business for some time, taking time for this activity reflects your choice to review your business from a position of strength.

This evaluation will help you objectively evaluate what your service business needs, as well as its strengths and weaknesses, so you are able to create a more solid foundation from which to grow. You will find this Business Evaluation activity valuable if you are:

- Developing an idea for a new service business or for a new facet of an existing one
- In the beginning stages of a new service business
- Rethinking or reorganizing an existing service business
- Wanting to move to another level of success.

The functions and activities identified in this section are typical for individuals in service businesses. Some may not apply to your business, such as bonding or liability insurance. In addition, there may be questions you have not yet considered and still others that you will not be able to answer. Most questions contain a reference to the section in this manual where the related activity is covered. Use these references to determine the appropriateness of an activity to your business.

You may feel overwhelmed as you evaluate these issues and determine which activities, details, and simple steps will help you develop your idea into a fully operating business. This is natural. The beginning of any new project requires commitment, organization, and perseverance. If you feel overwhelmed or resistant, take a break to get some distance from it, or answer Summary Question 2 on Page 18. Continue when you feel calm again.

Activity 4. Business Evaluation & Checklist

Refer to the Glossary (Appendix A) for definitions. As you answer the following questions, check the appropriate box, or enter a rating from 1-10.

■ MANAGEMENT

1. Do you have a working name for your business? (Activity 19, Question 2, Page 82.)

    a. Are you ready to choose a legal name for your business? (Activity 19, Question 2, Page 82.)

13

Empowering Vision

                                                                                                  YES / IN PROGRESS / NO / N/A

    b. If you are a sole proprietor or partnership, have you checked your state's Department of Revenue to determine if this business name is already being used? (Appendix C, Question 3.)

    c. If you answered yes to 1b, have you registered the name of your business with your state's Department of Revenue?

    d. If you are incorporating, have you contacted the Secretary of State to see if the name you have chosen is available? (Appendix C, Question 3.)

2. Are your long-term vision, purpose, function and goals clear? (Activity 1.)

3. Are your current goals clear? (Activity 2.)

4. Have you determined the benefits your service provides to your target clientele? (Activity 9.)

    a. Are you comfortable with your business image? (Activity 9.)

    b. Are you clear about the level of quality you will offer? (Activity 9.)

5. Is your income-generating program well developed? (Activity 11.)

6. Have you set your fees? (Activity 13.)

    a. Are your fees within reasonable limits for your service? (Activities 11, 13 and 17.)

    b. On the average, with a reasonable workload, does your business provide sufficient income to meet its overhead and your income needs? (Activities 11, 12, and 32.)

    c. Do you consistently reach or exceed your income needs? (Activity 5, Question 9, Page 22; Activity 11, Question 11, Page 41; and Activities 12 and 26.)

    d. Are you comfortable with the days and hours you perform your service? (Activity 12.)

	YES	IN PROGRESS	NO	N/A
7. Have you created a start-up cost budget? (Activity 5, Question 9d, Page 22.)				
a. Do you have access to the start-up capital necessary to create your business or develop a new program? (Activity 26 and Appendix B.)				
b. Have you calculated your business overhead expenses? (Activity 5, Question 9e, Page 23.)				
c. Have you created an operating budget? (Activity 5, Question 9f, Page 23; Activity 11, Question 11, Page 41; and Activity 26.)				
8. Have you developed payment policies and other written policies or contracts as appropriate? (Activity 14.)				
a. Do you know how to prepare an invoice for your clients? (Activity 13.)				
b. Do you know how to collect overdue payments from clients? (Activity 13 and Appendix C, Question 6, Page 187.)				
9. Have you allocated time for management and administrative activities? (Activities 6-8, 11, and 12.)				
10. Do you use a good filing system? (Activity 15.)				
11. Do you want to accept credit cards from your clients? If so, have you researched the necessary procedures? (Appendix C, Question 4, Page 186.)				

■ MARKETING

	YES	IN PROGRESS	NO	N/A
12. Do you know how to conduct market research? (Marketing Introduction, Page 63.)				
13. Have you created a profile of your ideal client? (Activity 16.)				
14. Have you analyzed your competition? (Activity 17.)				
15. Do you know which service industry includes your service? (Activity 18.)				
a. Do you know the growth stage of your service industry? (Activity 18.)				

Empowering Vision

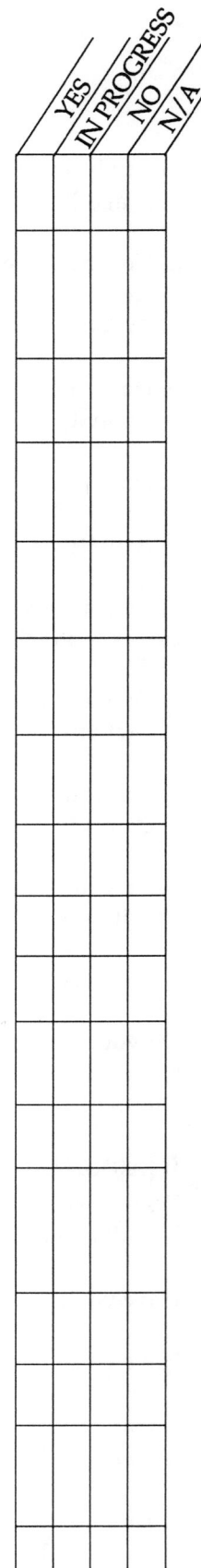

  b. Have you established your position in your service industry? (Activity 19.)

  c. Have you evaluated the possible external forces that could affect the stability of your business? (Activities 3, 18, and 19.)

  d. Does your business name include a slogan that states your position? (Activity 19.)

16. Have you considered all the ways you can promote your service? (Activity 20.)

  a. Do your promotional materials reflect your positioning objectives? (Activities 19 and 24.)

  b. Are you adequately using networking and free publicity and media opportunities for your business? (Activity 20.)

  c. Have you allocated adequate time for promotion? (Activities 6, 7, and 21.)

  d. Are you comfortable with selling? (Activity 22.)

  e. Do you have a basic sales presentation? (Activity 22.)

  f. Do you have a cover letter? (Activity 23.)

  g. Do you have a procedure for making sales calls? (Activity 22.)

  h. Have you created a promotion plan? (Activity 21.)

■ ACCOUNTING AND LEGAL

17. Does your bookkeeping system adequately serve your needs? (Activities 25-31 and 33.)

18. Do you have an accountant? (Financial Matters, Page 117.)

19. Do you have a lawyer? (Financial Matters, Page 119.)

20. Is your business properly licensed and legally registered? (Appendix C, Question 3, Page 185.)

21. Do you have a chart of accounts? (Activity 25.)

	YES	IN PROGRESS	NO	N/A

22. Are your receipts and disbursements journals up to date and accurate? (Activities 27 and 28.)

23. Do you need a petty cash accounting system? (Activity 33.)

24. Do you reconcile your bank statement monthly? (Activity 34.)

25. Do you create a Profit & Loss Statement regularly? (Activity 29.)

26. Do you prepare Balance Sheets and Variance Statements? (Activities 26, 29 and 30 and 31.)

27. Are all your tax payments current? (Taxes, Page 159.)

28. Do you need a business proposal to obtain capital for your business? See Appendix B.

29. Do you need to be bonded to offer your service? (Appendix C, Question 5, Page 186.)

30. Do you need to carry business insurance protection? (Appendix C, Question 5, Page 186.)

31. Do you need legal disclosure forms for clients? See your lawyer.

32. Does your business location adequately serve your needs? (Activity 9, Question 11, Page 35 and Activity 11, Question 8, Page 40.)

33. Is your location within legal and zoning requirements? (Appendix C, Question 3, Page 185.)

34. Do you plan to do business in other states? If so, have you checked with an attorney or an accountant to review out-of-state requirements and to discuss relevant legal and accounting issues? (Appendix C, Question 3, Page 185 and Question 8, Page 188.)

35. Do you know where to find more information on these and other business issues? (Appendix C, Question 7, Page 187, and Question 8, Page 188.)

Empowering Vision

Summary

If you answered "no" or "in progress" to any of the previous questions, you have identified activities and legal requirements of doing business that you may need to complete. Refer to the activities and questions suggested, review your answers, then list what you need to do or check on, along with projected completion dates. Add them to the appropriate track on your CPM Chart, the time management tool in Activity 6.

1. How have your ideas, perceptions, or feelings about your business developed or changed since you answered these questions? What are you prepared to do as a result?

2. Recall and describe the fears, resistances, or limiting patterns that you experienced while completing this activity. List them in priority order and explain what you are ready to do about them.

3. Reflect on the important points in this activity and describe how you feel empowered.

◆

Like these road signs, that safely regulate the flow of traffic, law, policies and procedures regulate business. Understanding them brings a secure journey.

Section 1. Management

Organizing and Planning Your Business

Now that you have envisioned your preferred lifestyle and evaluated your strengths and limiting patterns, you are ready to organize, or reorganize, your business. Even if your business is already established, you will find this activity valuable for discovering the unknown, forgotten or ignored details that may be inhibiting even more success.

From the Empowering Vision perspective, the service you provide is your art. The business functions of Program Development and Implementation, Marketing, Management, and Public Relations are the media that will transform your creative expression into the viable service business you envision. Every artist, no matter what their medium, knows the exhilaration of expressing an inner, creative vision with the clarity that comes from experience and trust. The same is true of business. Know your business, and you will succeed in creating the lifestyle you want through the service you love.

Activity 5, Organizing Your Business, is essential if you are just beginning to develop your service into an income-generating business. Or, if you are already in business, this activity will help you evaluate, reorganize, and streamline your business by revealing its strengths and weaknesses. With this information, you can make solid, empowering choices.

This activity will help you understand that planning is an exciting, creative process that begins with vision and becomes reality through a sequence of simple, understandable steps of your own choosing. Because people typically resist details and planning, you may feel resistance. If so, consider the following suggestions:

- If even the thought of working with details raises resistance, answer Question 11, Page 23, before beginning this activity. As you begin to understand the source of your resistance, it becomes easier to do what you know is right for yourself and your business.

- Call upon your mentor for support. Consider asking someone to do this activity with you. Two minds will flow more easily than one.

- During the planning stage, it is easiest to think each idea through completely before thinking about the next one. In a brainstorming process, begin by listing everything your business needs and doesn't have. Think in terms of items and activities (i.e., a new computer, a new business card, a brochure); then organize all activities and purchases or acquisitions into a plan that outlines the steps you are ready to take to create your desired result.

- Do the planning activities slowly and thoughtfully. As always, answer only the questions you feel comfortable with, and if you begin to feel overwhelmed or resistant, do something else for a while. If you do take a break, be aware of your thoughts and feelings. You may want to answer Question 11 to evaluate the source of your discomfort. When you are ready to continue, begin by reviewing the answers to the questions you completed. Continue from where you stopped.

- Carefully read through the rest of the visioning and planning activities. To develop confidence, do the easy activities first. Then, when you are more relaxed and confident, complete the activities that trigger resistance.

Success in business results from clarity, commitment, and perseverance—the natural consequences of clear vision, careful planning and follow-through. To experience the success you described in your vision, you will want to replace your resistance and limitations with supportive, empowering patterns. And there is another gift from planning: the activities in this manual culminate in your promotion plan—the plan of action through which you reach your clients and generate income.

Activity 5. Organizing Your Business

1. **Identify Business Requirements.** Begin by making a master list of all the necessities—items, activities, and projects—required for your business that you have not yet acquired or accomplished. List them as you think of them, from small details such as supplies, to large projects such as planning a seminar. Don't create confusion by being too specific with fine details, such as calculating the number of pencils you will use in a month. Just list "pencils."

    The following list will help you begin.

Advertising copy - camera ready	Dictionary, thesaurus
Answering machine or service	Equipment
Appointment book	Fee Schedule
Assistant	Filing system & supplies
Bills - system for paying	Furniture
Bonding	Insurance
Bookkeeping system	Licenses
Break-even calculation	Market needs analysis
Brochure	Marketing strategy
Budgets: start-up and operating	Networking plan
Business cards, letterhead, envelopes	Office or business location
Business image and logo	Office supplies
Business name (registered)	Policies and payment contract
Business plan	Postage
Checking account	Program outline
Client profile	Program research and design
Computer and software	Promotion plan
Continuing education	Research on competition
Cover letter	Resource and educational materials
Desk	Sales presentation

Section 1. Management

Start-up capital	Time management system
Support network	Trade name registration
Tax calculation and payment system	Vision and goals
Telephone	Work Schedule

2. **Assign Initial Priorities.** Within a time frame appropriate for you, consider the importance of each item on your master list, using these designations:

   A - Immediate   **B** - Short term   **C** - Long term

   Determine a date for each designation with your time structure. For example, A could be 11/1; B could be 12/15; and C could be 1/15 and so on. Write the appropriate date next to each designation.

3. **Label Business Function Lists.** Label separate pages with the business functions that follow, and divide each page into A, B, and C sections. If you are not sure about which of the following categories to use, think about whether the item or activity helps with planning, organization and administration, promotion, or with the design and implementation of your income-generating program. Including your personal activities in your time planning is optional. If you have many personal activities, you may want to include a personal track.

   Program Development and Implementation: includes design, research, and implementation of your service into an income-generating program; also includes continuing education. (Use Activity 11 to plan your program in depth.)

   Marketing: includes market research and all promotional activities you will use to sell your service. (Activities 16-24 are for developing your marketing strategy.)

   Management: includes licensing, legal, insurance, planning and office needs, budgeting, funding, accounting, tax planning, personnel—all the details that maintain your business. (Activities 25-34 are for setting up your accounting records.)

   Public Relations: includes professional contacts and group associations, public speaking, press releases, and media coverage you may utilize to gain credibility and exposure. (Activity 20 provides guidance in initiating these activities.)

   Personal [optional]: includes vacations, exercise and workout routines, doctor's appointments, out-of-town guests; in short, those major events and regular activities in your personal life that affect your schedule.

4. **Create Business Function Lists.** Transfer items, activities and projects from your master list to the A, B, or C section of the appropriate business function list. Remember that if you are unclear about the appropriate business category, consider how the item in question will affect your business. Whatever you decide, be consistent. As you transfer these, use an asterisk (*) to mark the ones that are complex projects involving numerous steps. Add new ideas to your master list as they occur to you. Then transfer and mark them as appropriate.

5. **Add Visioning Goals.** Evaluate Questions 3-5 from Activity 2, Current Vision, and add the appropriate goals and ideas to your function lists. Include dates and costs, as appropriate.

6. **Add Learning Goals.** Review Activity 3, Self-Evaluation, Questions 7 and 11 and add relevant ideas. Review Activity 4, Business Evaluation and transfer activities that are marked "no" or "in progress" to the A, B, or C category of the appropriate business function list.

7. **Set Completion Dates and Estimate Costs.** As appropriate, add the costs and approximate dates by which you will complete each activity or project and acquire each item. Be realistic in your expectations. By including dates and costs, you are taking the first step toward effective time management and determining your start-up and basic overhead costs.

8. **Establish Priorities.** You will transfer projects and activites to your CPM Chart (see Activity 6, Critical Path Method, Question 7). To plan complex projects, use the Planning Chart on Page 33 to list the sequence of steps necessary for its completion.

    To assist in organizing complex projects, label each project step with A, B, or C as in Question 2. The C items may, in time, become As: For example, "Preparing your notes for a class" may be a C this week; sometime before your class, it will become an A. Some Cs will drop off your list as you discover you are no longer interested in them. The Bs will become either As or Cs and should be addressed as appropriate.

> *"There is only one problem,*
> *namely our resistance to seeing things as they are,*
> *or more accurately, seeing the wholeness as it is."*
> Willis Harmon

9. **Other Start-up Activities.** At the pace and times right for you, finish organizing your business by completing these start-up activities:

    a. Choose the income-generating program you are ready to develop and promote. If needed, use Activity 10, Narrowing Your Focus, for assistance in choosing the right program to develop now.

    b. Plan your program by completing Activity 11, Program Planning and Development.

    c. To determine the number of clients you can serve and the number that will provide your required income, complete Activity 12, Projecting Your Ideal Workload.

    d. Prepare your start-up budget by calculating the actual costs for the items on your function lists. Set dates and add the figures to your operating budget (see 9f below). Consider whether you currently have the money for these; whether you will need to delay or eliminate some costs; or whether you will borrow the money required.

    e. Calculate your monthly overhead—the recurring operating expenses of your business. Remember that overhead costs do not relate specifically to your income-generating programs but to the general costs of doing business. Overhead includes such expenses as rent, utilities, telephone, business cards, and office supplies. To determine monthly overhead, review the Budget Worksheet in Activity 26, Budget, and select the appropriate items.

    f. Complete your operating budget, including overhead, program income and expenses, using Activity 26, Budget.

10. **Organize a Filing System for Your Records.** For guidance, see Activity 15, Organizing Your Filing System.

11. What are your feelings about organization and planning? Describe how these feelings support or limit you. If you feel resistance to organization and planning, explain why. What are you ready to do as a result?

12. In retrospect, what do you recognize to be your strengths with regard to organization, planning, and details?

13. What more are you ready to learn and develop regarding organization, planning, and details? What internal and external resources will you draw upon? List the steps you will take, in order of priority, and add dates when appropriate. How can your mentors and support network help you?

◆

Empowering Vision

Managing Your Time

On some days, it may seem that there is not enough time to accomplish everything. Yet, you can experience harmony with the flow of your daily activities. All you need is clarity, thoughtful decision-making, and careful planning. A carefully designed time plan will align your business and personal activities. As you follow your plan, monitoring and adjusting it as necessary, your business will have a strong, vital life, and you will have fun.

The Critical Path Method (CPM) was developed by the construction industry to minimize cash requirements and maximize efficiency, labor, and storage capacity. The method staggers delivery of materials according to the production schedule, thus ensuring, for example, that insulation materials won't be rained on while the foundation is poured.

Our simplified version is an invaluable tool for integrating your business functions with your personal activities. The method is also useful for planning projects with specific completion dates.

The CPM facilitates efficient and cost-effective planning. By looking at your projected completion date, thinking through the steps from completion back to the present, then planning from the present forward to the completion date, you are evaluating your plans as a whole. Creating the CPM Chart allows you to place all the activities in time, so they can be completed with an efficient use of your resources—time, energy, money, and people.

Developing your CPM Chart will enable you to think an idea through from conception to completion—on paper—before you take action. This will ensure a successful and timely completion of all activities, as well as eliminate the waste and chaos that result from unnecessary mistakes. The CPM is the realistic time line that supports a wholesome lifestyle with built-in flexibility for unforeseen events.

Create a CPM Chart to:

- Organize yourself through periods of change or high-level activity
- Organize and schedule on-going business activities
- Develop and plan a new project or income-generating program
- Bring more strength and integrity to your business management.

To create your CPM Chart, review your business and program activities, as listed in Activity 5, Question 8, and Activity 11, Question 9. Decide if your CPM Chart will be for one project. If so, determine the completion date. If you are using it to plan and schedule all your business activities, design your CPM Chart for two- or three-month increments.

In designing your CPM Chart, place all activities sequentially along your time line, from the present to completion. This will help you determine if your proposals harmonize with your on-going activities. If not, the CPM Chart will help you decide which adjustments to make. Your CPM Chart also lets you preview the possible effects of making changes and adding new projects. For example, if you have a proposal due in six weeks, you can see that it will be easier to plan relocating your office after the due date.

Again, if you are resistant to planning, ask someone close to you to help you create your CPM Chart. Consider, also, completing Question 12, Page 27, to better understand the source of your resistance. At minimum, consider using the scheduling tools discussed in Activities 7 and 8.

> *"Time is the scarcest resource, and unless it is managed,*
> *nothing else can be managed."*
> Peter Drucker

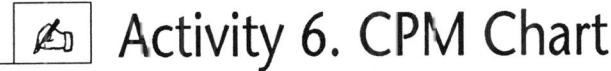 Activity 6. CPM Chart
Time Management: Using the Critical Path Method

Note: Refer to the sample CPM Chart on Page 28 as you read the following instructions. Use a pencil and a good eraser.

1. On poster board or a large piece of paper (the larger the better), use a ruler to divide the paper in half by drawing a thin double line from the left margin to the right. This is the time line, known as the "critical path."

2. The business functions from Activity 5, Question 3, will each become a track on your CPM Chart: Program Development and Implementation, Marketing, Management, Public Relations, and, if you choose, Personal. If needed, you can change the titles to fit your needs. To accommodate these, draw a vertical line from top to bottom to create a space wide enough to write the functions in.

3. Draw a horizontal line to divide the upper half of the CPM Chart into two equal tracks. If you choose to include a Personal track, divide the lower half into three tracks; if not, create two. Or, create a category that fits your specific needs.

4. At the left margin, write Program Development and Implementation in the top track, and Marketing in the track just below it. Then write the remaining business functions in the subtracks below the double line, beginning with Public Relations and ending with Personal, if applicable. (See sample on Page 28.)

You can subdivide each track into two or three subtracks (see sample) by drawing horizontal lines from the left margin to the right margin and/or color coding the various programs. If you choose to subdivide the tracks, subtitle them in the left margin as appropriate. Do what is best for your needs. The point is to place the activities for each program along the same horizontal line so you can easily see the sequence of activities for each program and business function.

Empowering Vision

5. Each of these business function tracks will contain the ongoing activities you listed in Activity 5, Organizing Your Business, as well as activities you will list in Activity 11, Program Planning and Development. If you have two or more income-generating programs, you can color code the activities in each program to make your CPM Chart easier to use.

6. Choose whether to begin your CPM Chart on the first or the fifteenth day of the month prior to today's date, and complete it two months from that date. Or, begin it today and end it on the date, several months from now, that you have set to complete the project.

   Write the appropriate beginning date on the timeline at the left margin and the completion date on the line at the right margin. At midpoint, write the date exactly between your beginning and completion dates. Between midpoint and both margins, add 8s and 22s to provide an easy-to-read, weekly progression. Dates along the top and bottom of the page can provide an additional guide, especially if you have a large piece of paper. Use pencil, so you can erase.

7. Review your business function lists from Activity 5, Question 3. If you haven't created these categories yet, do so now. Taking one function at a time, transfer the items with dates to the appropriate track on the CPM Chart. Use samll sticky pads or write directly on the paper.

   Describe each item in abbreviated terms and draw a box around it. Include the completion date in the upper right corner. At the bottom left corner, write the number of hours each activity will take. List activities that are milestones, rather than minute tasks. For example, see sample CPM Chart for COMPLETE BROCHURE COPY on the 7th. You probably don't need to include WRITE PARA. 1 on the 6th, and so forth.

   For projects with sequenced steps, write the steps along the same horizontal line, above or below the appropriate dates. (On the sample CPM Chart, see the row of boxes above the timeline that illustrate the schedule for producing a brochure.)

8. Look through your appointment book for scheduled appointments and events. Add these to the appropriate track. Include repetitive tasks and activities that require a substantial amount of time and that affect your schedule. Adjust dates as necessary. Remember to allow for unforeseen events that could create delays. Remember to allow for unforeseen events that could create delays. Be realistic with your expectations. If other people will help with certain items and activities, write their initials next to the item.

9. When all activities have been listed, evaluate your CPM Chart both horizontally and vertically to see if your plans are realistic. Are there any periods of intense activity and possible stress? If so, ask yourself if you are willing to handle the excess. If you are, begin adjusting your attitude and current plans accordingly. When the time arrives you will be ready, and the resulting peace of mind will be your reward. If you are not willing to experience the extra work and stress, rearrange your plans.

10. Transfer CPM activities to your appointment book. When adjusting or adding to your CPM Chart, be sure to adjust the corresponding information in your appointment book.

Section 1. Management

11. Evaluate each track. Is one active while another is sparse? Determine why. Do the active tracks reflect activities that clearly support your business? Does the function with limited activity reflect resistance and inattentiveness that could undermine your business? For example, if you are seeing so many clients that you do not have time for bookkeeping, are you falling behind in your books? Are you over-networking (with little obvious return) and under-promoting? Evaluate the tracks and make adjustments as needed.

12. Recall and describe the fears, resistance or self-limiting patterns that you experienced while completing this activity. List them in order of priority and explain what you are ready to do about them.

13. How did this activity affect your enthusiasm for your business? Explain how this information will bring you more stability.

14. Reflect on the important points in this exercise and describe how you feel empowered. How will your CPM Chart aid you during periods of intense activity, stress or change?

15. In retrospect, what do you realize you already knew about time management?

16. What must you learn and develop with regard to time management? List the resources you are ready to draw upon and the steps you will take, including dates when appropriate.

Prepare a new CPM Chart several weeks before the ending date of the current one. After you are comfortable with scheduling your time more efficiently, you may choose to create a CPM Chart only during especially busy periods, when you want to complete a new project in a specified time, or when you want to integrate a new program into your ongoing activities. Eventually, you may prefer to use only one or two tracks rather than all four or five.

If you choose not to use the CPM Chart, you can use Activity 7, Master Schedule, and Activity 8, Planning Chart, to assist you in organizing your activities. Although each of the tools stands alone, they form an effective time management system when used in conjunction with the CPM Chart.

◆

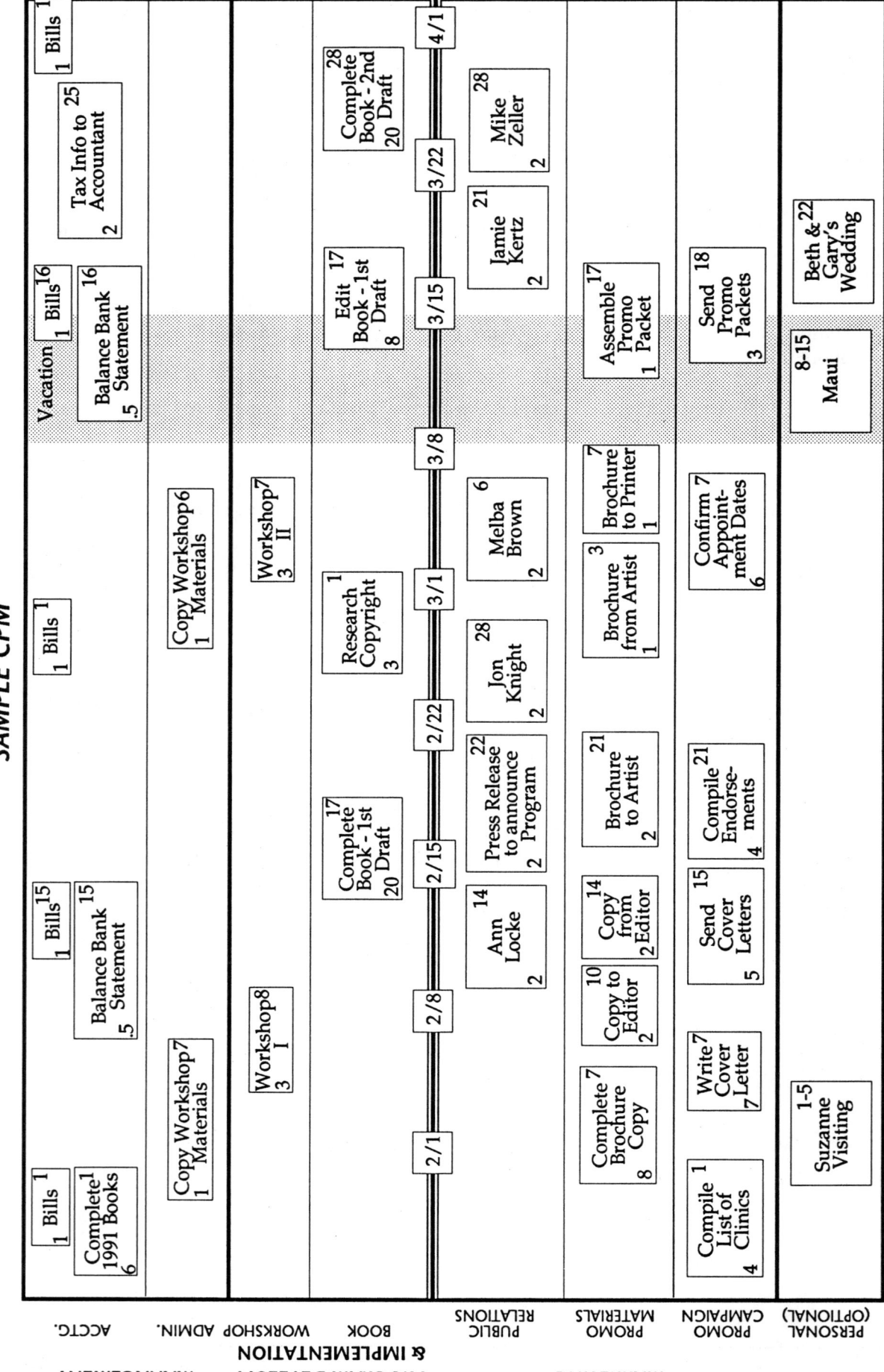

Section 1. Management

Your Typical Work Week

The Master Schedule provides a picture of your typical work week. When you do all the business functions yourself, it is especially important to design a schedule that allows you to be at your best for each type of activity. Keep in mind your own cycles and rhythms, as well as the business hours of related business services, your clients' schedules, and recurring events, such as meetings, errands, and personal activities.

✍ Activity 7. Master Schedule

Note: Copy the form on Page 31 and study the sample on Page 30.

1. Review your appointment book for scheduled and typical activities and times. List all your regularly scheduled clients, meetings, classes, and so forth, at the appropriate times on the Master Schedule.

2. Mark out times that you are available for providing your income-producing service.

    Note: If your business accepts rush jobs, to accomodate your fluctuation in schedule, reduce the number of hours in your schedule accordingly. For example, if you average eight rush work hours per week, you might schedule only four days, or leave several hours each day unscheduled. Or, consider using a contract worker to help with the overload.

3. Mark out time for activities such as planning, promotion and networking, and for ongoing administrative tasks such as returning telephone calls, reading mail, organizing your desk, filing, paying bills, and bookkeeping. Make sure these reflect the times when you are at your best for each.

4. Mark out times for personal activities you do during your work time, such as exercising, picking up the kids, etc.

5. Review Activity 5, Organizing Your Business; Activity 11, Program Planning and Development; and Activity 12, Projecting Your Ideal Workload. Include all your activities. When you complete Activity 21, Promotion Plan, transfer promotion activities to your schedule.

6. Review your Master Schedule. Does everything fit easily? If not, determine the adjustments you are prepared to make. Before agreeing to new clients or activities, evaluate your Master Schedule to see how you can comfortably allocate the time involved.

◆

SAMPLE MASTER SCHEDULE FORM

	Monday	Tuesday	Wednesday	Thursday	Friday	Saturday
7:00 7:30 8:00 8:30 9:00 9:30 10:00 10:30 11:00 11:30 12:00 12:30	Research new program Exercise	Clients Lunch	Breakfast with Intern Group Bookkeeping Exercise	Clients Lunch	Clients Group Exercise	Workshop
1:00 1:30 2:00 2:30 3:00 3:30 4:00 4:30 5:00 5:30 6:00	Write article	Clients	Admin. activities	Promotional activites - workshop, brochure, handouts, telephone calls, etc.	OFF Networking	
6:30 7:00 7:30 8:00 8:30 9:00		Continuing Education Class	Board Meeting 2nd Wed.	Group		

MASTER SCHEDULE FORM

Make copies of this form and use it as an original.

	Monday	Tuesday	Wednesday	Thursday	Friday	Saturday
7:00						
7:30						
8:00						
8:30						
9:00						
9:30						
10:00						
10:30						
11:00						
11:30						
12:00						
12:30						
1:00						
1:30						
2:00						
2:30						
3:00						
3:30						
4:00						
4:30						
5:00						
5:30						
6:00						
6:30						
7:00						
7:30						
8:00						
8:30						
9:00						

© Empowering Vision

Empowering Vision

Planning Chart

The Planning Chart is a simple tool for time management and project organization. With six separate boxes, you can organize projects either by days of the week or weeks of the month. Or you can create global "to do" lists for projects, activities or business functions. Some possibilities are:

- A weekly listing of the projects and activities you intend to accomplish each day
- A monthly listing of the projects and activities for each week
- One project with as many as six steps, listing the sub-steps
- Up to six different projects and their component steps
- Each business function and its ongoing activities
- A weekly listing of activities such as telephone calls, letters, computer projects, errands, accounting, etc.

Activity 8. Planning Chart

Make copies of the blank worksheet on Page 33.

1. Evaluate the above options and determine how the Planning Chart can best serve you.

2. Monthly/Weekly Planning: Fill in boxes #1-6 with the names of the appropriate days (Monday-Saturday) or weeks (Week of ____). Determine the projects and activities you intend to accomplish. In the first box, list the activities for that period; include dates. Evaluate your CPM Chart and appointment book for each period to determine whether it is possible to complete all the activities listed. If not, make adjustments.

3. Global "To Do" Lists: Evaluate the Global "To do" ideas above and determine which will serve your needs now. Fill in boxes #1-6 with the names of specific projects or activities. In each box, list the necessary tasks. If the project is large, for example—create promotion plan—divide it into steps: identify clientele, research competition, create promotion budget, create brochure, etc. Include dates.

4. When you have completed the Planning Chart, indicate times on your CPM Chart, your Master List, and in your appointment book to accomplish each activity. Evaluate whether everything fits comfortably. If not, revise as needed.

5. How will using the Planning Chart aid you in your daily management?

◆

© Empowering Vision

PLANNING CHART
Make copies of this form and use it as an original.

_____
(title of project, if applicable)

#1 _____   #2 _____   #3 _____

#4 _____   #5 _____   #6 _____

\# = months or specific project

Clarifying Your Service, Quality, and Professional Image

From the Empowering Vision perspective, your service is the foundation and intention of your business. It is your gift to the world around you. It is the benefit you provide through your business.

For example, a person who wants to see people more relaxed might choose to become a massage therapist, biofeedback technician, yoga instructor, or meditation teacher. The *service* is to help people relax; the income-generating *program* is either massage, biofeedback consultation, yoga, or meditation classes.

Visualize yourself standing with another person in an elevator. You begin talking, and the other person asks you what you do. Since you want your response to combine your service and program, you begin by stating your service. "I help people relax." Then, you add the description of your program, "by teaching meditation." Once you have created a statement that clearly explains what you offer, state it the same way to everyone.

Think of your statement this way. Medieval merchants attracted customers by hanging signs that advertised their service in front of their shops. Your professional image is similar to those signs. People who are ready to buy your service are attracted to you through the professional image you project.

Clarify your service and the quality you want to deliver. Then, develop your image to reflect these. Until these are defined, the "sign" in front of your shop will look blurry to passers-by, who probably won't take the time to come in. When your service and professional image are clearly in focus, people will recognize this and begin to turn to you.

Once you have clearly identified your image, incorporate it into every facet of your business: your actions, personal appearance, work surroundings, and promotional materials.

*"Deep within you is everything perfect,
ready to radiate through you and out into the world."*
Accept This Gift

✍ Activity 9. Your Service, Quality, & Image

1. Briefly describe your service. Begin by looking beyond the mechanics of what you actually do to determine what you want to give others. For example, a massage therapist may want to help people reduce their stress, relax, or eliminate pain; a writer may want to provide straightforward editing or a translation service. Condense your description into one strong service statement.

2. Why do you want to offer this service? What personal need does it satisfy? Why is this important to you?

3. Describe the need in society that your service satisfies.

4. Describe your service's evolutionary purpose—the intention for which it is directed to effect change. (See also Evolutionary Need in the Glossary.)

> *"I believe that every right
> implies a responsibility,
> every opportunity, an obligation;
> every possession, a duty."*
> John D. Rockefeller, Jr.

5. In one word statements or short phrases, list the needs your service satisfies—the benefits—for your typical client. Why does each need exist? Review your list and choose four or five of the most important.

6. What does your service provide that is different, unique, or not yet available from other services like it?

7. On a scale of 1-10 (ten being the highest), what level of quality are you ready to offer through your service? Why? What is its current level? If there is a discrepancy between the two, explain. Describe and explain what you are ready to do to offer this level of quality. What skills must you develop along the way?

8. What is your desired professional image? What image are you presently projecting? What is lacking or inconsistent? What are you ready to do about it?

9. Do you like the image projected by your promotional materials? Do you have the money and professional expertise to create the professional image you want? If not, what will you do to enhance your image?

10. Does your current location adequately serve your needs? Does it fit with your desired image?

Empowering Vision

11. Reflect on the life experience (personal and professional) that prepared you to offer this service. Consider, especially, the challenging and difficult situations that have led you to this service. Write a brief biography.

12. Recall and describe the fears, resistances, or self-limiting patterns that you experienced while completing this activity. List them in order of priority and explain what you will do about them.

13. Reflect on the important points this activity revealed to you and describe the clarity you have gained. Describe how this will affect your professional image and the quality of your service. Are you uncomfortable with any of these responses? Explain. How can your mentors and support network help you?

◆

The words that describe your service give a visual and mental impression of what you do.

36

Section 1. Management

Choosing Your Income-Generating Program

Most people, when first self-employed, experience a mixture of excitement and fear. A fairly universal response is to think of many ways to earn income, usually more ways than one person can easily organize, plan, capitalize, and promote. If you are experiencing this, you will want to stop and reflect on your options. You will limit confusion and demands on your time, energy, and resources by developing and promoting only one—at the most two—new programs at a time.

An essential skill for any new manager is the ability to stay centered and focused on one income-producing program. (In this course, a program is defined as one component of a service.) For example, a therapist may have three programs: individual therapy, group therapy, and workshops. Each program is evaluated separately because each may serve different clientele, require a different marketing strategy, and even different promotional materials. After one program is successfully developed, it's time to shape and implement the others.

The following activity, Narrowing Your Focus, assists you in clarifying the income-producing program you are ready to develop. Use Activity 10 to choose the program appropriate for your unique circumstances. It will help you visualize and select the program that will provide the service that you want to offer and that your target clientele wants to buy.

Note: If you are certain of the program you are ready to develop, skip Activity 10 and do Activity 11, Program Planning and Development.

Activity 10. Narrowing Your Focus

1. From Activity 9, Your Service, Quality, & Image, state your basic service in one sentence.

2. List all the income-generating ideas you have been considering that will help you fulfill your service as stated in Question 1.

3. In order to begin narrowing your list of possible progams to one you will develop, begin by considering the following points and ideas:

    - If you want to increase your income, identify the program idea in Question 2 that will generate the highest income while utilizing the least amount of time, energy, and money.

    - If you want your next program to satisfy needs other than financial, evaluate the following list and write down one or two goals you want your next program to fulfill:

Empowering Vision

variety	different clientele	excitement	skill development
satisfaction	greater visibility	exposure	fun
empowerment	service	creativity	relationship

- Add several of your own that fulfill your unique and current professional goals.

4. With your goals from Question 3 in mind, use a 1-10 scale to rate your list of income-producing ideas.

5. Cross off all ideas rated 8 or less. Of the remaining ideas, number them in order of importance, based on your excitement, willingness, skill and readiness with each. Which one(s) have the highest rating? Why? Are you clear about your program choice now? If yes, do Activity 11. If not, continue with Question 6.

6. Begin with the program idea that has the highest rating and remember your Life Purpose Vision. Imagine your personal and professional life several years from now. Which program idea fits with your life as you want it? Explain how you think you will feel at the end of your life if you have not developed this idea to its potential. Why do you want to offer this program?

Note: If this is the program you are ready to develop, continue with the following questions. If not, repeat Question 6 using the program idea with next highest rating. Continue repeating Question 5 with each program idea until you choose one.

7. If you were a prospective client, would you pay for this service? Explain.

8. Describe how this program will help create your Life Purpose Vision and your Current Vision.

9. Are you 100 percent ready to do this program now? If not, what do you need to do to be ready?

10. Recall and describe the fears, resistances or self-limiting patterns you experienced while completing this activity. List them in order of priority and explain what you will do about them.

11. Reflect on the important points this activity revealed to you and the clarity you have gained. How will this affect the quality of your service and your choice of program?

◆

*"People who can make good decisions
are some of the most sought-after people
in American business."*
Charles A. Coonradt

Section 1. Management

Developing Your Income-Generating Program

Note: Refer to the definitions of program on Page 37 and in the Glossary.

In the following activity, Program Planning and Development, you will develop an income-generating program for the segment of society that has identified a desire or need for your service. This program should pay for itself and assist you in providing your basic business overhead and personal income.

The process of transforming a creative idea into an income-generating program may seem monumental, yet even mountains can be moved by shifting a few rocks each day. With commitment to clear and careful planning, your service will have a solid share of the market in the community you choose to serve.

As stated in Activity 10, it is easiest and most effective to develop one program at a time, especially when you are working on your own. However, if you choose to plan more than one program, address them one at a time, using Activity 11. Begin by working with the program you chose in Activity 10.

Future Planning: After your program has stabilized and is self-generating, use this activity again to plan and further develop subsequent programs.

Product Planning: Although this course is designed for service businesses rather than production of goods, you may want to develop products, such as books or tapes, to complement your service. Since the same planning elements are involved, you can use this activity if you substitute "product" for "program."

"All that I give is given to myself."
Course In Miracles

Activity 11. Program Planning & Development

Note: If you feel overwhelmed, confused or resistant at any point during this activity, complete Question 12, enjoy a break, and begin again when you feel ready.

1. **Title and Purpose.** Write the title of this program and, in one sentence, state its purpose.

2. **Motivation and Personal Gain.** Explain your reasons for offering this program. What do you want to gain? Be honest.

3. **Social Need.** State the social need this program satisfies.

Empowering Vision

4. **Client State.** Describe this program's typical client. Describe the client's current state—how she or he is now—then how she or he will develop after experiencing your program.

5. **Benefits.** Using single words or short phrases, list the benefits your client will receive. Review your list, then choose the best four or five.

6. **Schedule.**

   a. In this program, determine the maximum, minimum, and optimum number of sessions (consulting hours or workshop sessions, for example) of this program per period (a period may be a week, month, season, quarter, or year).

   b. How many clients will you serve per session—maximum, minimum, and average? (See Activity 12.)

   c. Based on the number of clients you will serve, prepare a schedule indicating when you will offer your program. (See Activity 7.) Do some research to determine when sales for your type of service tend to be especially high and low.

7. **Program Outline.** Prepare an outline that describes your program. Include the number of sessions, the duration of each session, and as appropriate, the format for each session. Include a description of possible variations.

8. **Location.** Briefly describe the location(s) at which you will offer this program, including the internal set-up, and the surrounding environment. Evaluate whether your current location adequately serves your needs and is compatible with your business image. Do you prefer to find another location? Will your overhead increase if you do? By how much? Determine how you can enhance your current location if you choose to remain where you are.

9. **Program Organization.**

   a. **Identify Program Requirements.** Make a master list of all the items, activities and projects required for this program that you have not yet acquired and accomplished. Include essential steps, information, market research, resources, personnel, materials, equipment, promotional materials, supports, and so forth. Refer to Activity 5, Question 1 for guidance.

   b. **Assign Initial Priorities.** On your master list, within the time frame appropriate for this program, determine the importance of each item, using the following designations:
   A - Immediate   B - Short term   C - Long term

   c. **Label Program Requirements Lists.** Label two separate pages with "Program Development" and "Program Management," and divide each page into A, B, and C sections:

Section 1. Management

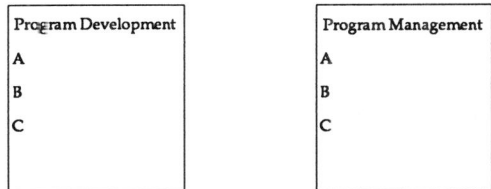

- Program Development includes the design, research, and implementation of your income-generating program.

- Program Management is everything else—logistical, administrative, and marketing.

d. **Create Program Requirements Lists.** Transfer items, activities and projects from your master list to the A, B, or C section of the appropriate program requirements list. Mark complex projects with an asterisk (*). Leave the one-step projects and one-time activities unmarked. Add new ideas to your master list as they occur to you, and transfer them to these lists as appropriate.

e. **Add Remaining Activities.** Refer to Question 8, Activity 5, Organizing Your Business, and add items, activities and projects from your Program Development and Implementation requirements list.

f. **Establish Priorities.** On each list, organize the A projects and items according to priority. For each project, use the Planning Chart from Page 33 to list the steps necessary for completion.

*"Until intelligent thought is linked
with appropriate action and follow-through,
there is no real accomplishment."*
Denis Waitley

g. **Set Target Dates and Estimate Costs.** As appropriate, add costs and the approximate dates by which you will acquire each item or complete each activity or project. If you want other people to help, include their initials.

Be realistic with your intentions. Compare the dates of these activities with your ongoing activities, and with the dates in your appointment book, as well as those scheduled from Activity 5. Will your plans work? Make adjustments as needed. Leave space for afterthoughts.

10. **Fees.** Determine the fee for this program. Outline retainer, deposit and payment arrangements. (See Activity 13.)

11. **Program Viability.** The following steps will help you evaluate the financial viability of your program.

a. **Program Income.** Review Question 7b to determine the maximum, minimum, and average number of clients you can serve per session. Multiply each of these figures by your fee. Using the average number of clients and the number of sessions you will offer per period, estimate the expected payment dates and amounts of income for the period you choose. Using the Budget Worksheet from Activity 26, list the gross income you project each month.

b. **Program Expenses.** Referring to Activity 5, Questions 7 and 9d, e and f, list the costs of organizing and maintaining your program. Transfer these to your Budget Worksheet for the months you expect them to occur.

c. **Promotional Expenses.** Multiply your program income (Question 11a) by 5 percent and include on your Budget Worksheet as promotional expenses. If you know the exact promotional costs, list the exact costs. As you complete your promotion plan (Activities 19-21), this figure may change.

d. **Business Overhead.** Add your business overhead expenses (as calculated in Activity 5, Organizing Your Business, Question 9e) to your Budget Worksheet for the period. If you have only one program, add all your projected overhead expenses to this program's expenses.

If you have more than one program, use Activity 12, Question 8, to calculate the percentage of your annual income represented by each program. For example, if you have three programs that contribute equally to your total business, include 33 percent—or one-third of your overhead expenses—in each program's budget. If your programs contribute varying amounts of income, calculate the average percentage for each and include in each program's budget. Include the correct proportion of your overhead expenses by multiplying each overhead expense by the percentage for the program.

e. **Net Income.** When you subtract total expenses from gross income, what is the net income for this program each month?

f. **Break-even Analysis.** To determine the profitability of a new or current program, calculate its break-even point. At the break-even point, income and expenses are equal. Above this point, income exceeds expenses and you generate a profit. Below this point, expenses exceed income and you have a loss. For help calculating the break-even point, see Activity 32.

How many clients do you need to break even per month, period, or session?

g. Will you make a reasonable profit with these income and expense projections? If not, will you raise your fees, lower expenses, or both? Make adjustments as appropriate, and recalculate the break-even point until you are satisfied.

Section 1. Management

12. Recall and describe any overwhelming feelings, resistance or self-limiting patterns you experienced while doing this activity. Describe how these limit your stability and success. List in priority order and explain what you will do about them.

13. In retrospect, what do you recognize to be your strengths in program planning and development? How will these strengths help you be successful? Put this activity away for a few days.

14. Reflect on the clrity you gained from completing this activity and describe how you feel empowered.

15. After a few days, show your plan to someone who offers a program similar to yours, or to someone with solid business experience. Ask particularly about your time and expense estimates. Ask for feedback and suggestions. Take notes, add new ideas to your list, and integrate them into your plans.

16. Several days later, evaluate how this program aligns with your current goals. Determine whether its projected return will be worth the time, energy, and expense. Based on these answers, are you ready to develop it?

    a. If so, do Activity 6, Time Management, and, if needed, Activity 12, Projecting Your Ideal Workload, to plan the steps you listed in Question 9 above.

    b. If not, review Activity 10, choose another program, and complete this activity again.

You may use this activity to think through several income-generating ideas before you find one that satisfies your current goals. You have probably chosen to be self-employed, so you are free to make your own choices. By thinking through your business on paper, and by fine tuning your ideas, you will feel confident with your repetitive, day-to-day management activities. This will be reflected as profit on your financial statements.

Use this activity every time you begin a new program or project.

◆

*"If my business were organized with the intelligence
that orders the universe, my life would be
different in the following ways..."*
Marianne Weidlein

Evaluating Your Workload

When you sell a product, you can earn an income from it even when you are not working. However, when you provide a service, your income usually depends on how many hours you work, the number of clients you can serve, and the seasonal income flow of your service industry.

Business has its seasons—its ebbs and flows. Each industry that serves human needs and desires has its own unique periods of high and low purchasing. The flow of these periods depends upon the nature of the need or desire and upon how society relates it to other available services and products. For most service businesses, there will be abundant periods when the target clientele buys, periods when their purchasing attention is turned elsewhere, and periods of unpredictable and light demands.

Knowing the seasonal flows of your service industry will help you create the marketing strategy that best utilizes your resources. To be in sync with the flow, allocate promotion money for the beginning of the periods when your target clientele buys.

An understanding of these predictable cycles of demand will allow you to plan your activities—including vacations and research and development—to coincide with these slow periods. Familiarity with the cycles will also help you project and manage your cash flow accordingly. Further, you will be able to coordinate your promotional activities according to these seasonal fluctuations.

To determine your industry's financial cycles, begin by evaluating the financial effect of the following periods: Thanksgiving to New Year's (mid-November to early January); tax season (mid-March to the end of April); summer vacation (June through Labor Day) on your service.

Using this evaluation as a base, determine your industry's probable high and low financial periods. These will, in part, determine your busy and slow periods and, therefore, your cash flow.

As a service business manager, you should know how much work your business must generate to maintain your preferred income level, as well as provide basic overhead and profit for growth. As your business becomes better known and your service and reputation are established, the amount of work you obtain will increase and stabilize. By knowing just how much work you want and can handle, you can protect yourself from overload by contracting with others for assistance or referring clients to a colleague. You may also decide to take on a heavier workload for a time.

In addition, when you know your abilities and limits, you live without the restricted client flow that occurs when you fear overload. By focusing on your fears, you tend to realize them. At the same time, you have healthy limits that maintain your stability and integrity. A clear knowledge and acceptance of these, along with a willingness to release self-limiting patterns, will help you build a strong client base, as well as a free flow of clients.

Activity 12, Projecting Your Ideal Workload, will help you define your limits and answer these questions:

Section 1. Management

- How much time must I work to achieve my income goals? Do I want to work this amount of time?

- How much work am I able to handle? How much energy do I choose to expend? Does this amount of time fulfill my income goals? Should I subcontract or refer some of my work?

- What proportion of my available work hours do I need to allocate to unbillable, administrative time (preparing for clients, paying bills, running errands, etc.)?

- What are my industry's seasonal cycles? How can I effectively use slower periods for promoting, research, planning, vacationing, etc.?

Activity 12. Projecting Your Ideal Workload

Note: Begin by studying the Sample Work Scheduling Worksheet on Page 48, using the following instructions to guide you. The reference numbers on the chart correspond to question numbers in this activity.

Make a copy of the worksheet on Page 49 for your own calculations. Begin by writing the name of each of your programs on line 1 of the worksheet.

1. Across line 1, "PROGRAM," in columns A-D, write the names of your income-generating programs. You can use column D for a program or for miscellaneous items.

2. Determine your desired monthly gross income by adding together these amounts:

    - The minimum income you choose for your personal needs and debt repayment, if any
    - A reasonable cushion for the lifestyle you want
    - Quarterly tax payments
    - Business overhead costs (see Activity 5, Question 9e)
    - Program costs (see Activity 11, Question 11b, c, and d).

    Add 5 percent each for personal and business emergencies, another 5 percent each for whims and spontaneous ideas, and 10 percent for your IRA or personal savings.

3. Multiply your desired monthly gross income by 12 to get your desired gross annual income. Write this figure on line 14, column E. (On the sample worksheet, the annual figure is $48,000.)

4. In the annual cycle of your service industry, what are the seasonal high and low income periods? Evaluate your industry's high and low periods, and place a small X on lines 2-13 in columns A-D for the months that each of your programs is active. On the sample, Robert Johnson has scheduled workshops for April, August, and December (column A); intensives for

Empowering Vision

March and September (column B); family counseling for March, April, and October-December (column C); and group counseling for January, February, June, July, October, and November (column D).

5. In each box marked with an X, write the amount of income you project from that program.

6. Add the monthly income from columns A-D across, and write the total for each month in column E. Note that on the sample worksheet there is no income in May, but other months have much activity. If this occurs on your worksheet, determine if your income projections will allow you months without income. If not, you may need to reconsider your intention, rearrange your schedule, or work more in other months.

7. Total columns A-D vertically, to determine the annual income from each program and record the figures from each along line 14. Add the Annual Program totals along line 14, and write the total for these in Column E. This total should agree. (If not, check your math.)

8. Calculate the percentage of the total income each program provides by dividing your total annual income from line 14, column E, into the annual income for each program along line 14. Write the result for each on line 15. Be sure these total 100 percent. (In the sample, Program 4 is Group Counseling, which represents 40 precent of Johnson's income, or 40% x $48,000 = $19,200.)

9. In column F, lines 2-13, write the total number of hours you will need to implement each program for each month. Can you provide your service to this extent each month without feeling overwhelmed or reaching burnout? Will you need help to serve this many clients? If so, how will you create help? Total the hours for each month to determine the number of hours you will work annually, and write on line 15, column F. (616 is the number of annual work hours for our example.)

10. Evaluate your worksheet. Does your desired income reach your projected annual income? If not, you have not planned enough work to create your desired income, and you need to re-evaluate, reschedule, or raise your fees. How do your projected schedule and income look to you? How do they feel? Explain any concerns you have about coordinating your work schedule with the seasonal demands of your industry. What will you do to resolve these concerns? If needed, revise your projections until the schedule looks reasonable to you.

11. If you need help in your business, yet find yourself resisting help, is it because you:

    - Don't want to work with someone else?
    - Believe you should be able to do it yourself?
    - Feel no one else can do it as well as you can?
    - Think you can't afford it?
    - Don't have the time to train people?

    If you answered yes to any of these, you may be working against yourself. Reflect on this, and consider what you will do. Do you need to lower your income requirements? Can you raise

Section 1. Management

your hourly rate to decrease the number of clients or hours? Review your desired income figures and make adjustments to fit your abilities and circumstances. You can revise them once you have created stability through a strong client base and predictable cash flow.

12. Are you providing a program that you would like to discontinue but maintain because it is steady income? If so, use your worksheet to determine how and when you will be able to phase it out.

13. Describe the concerns or resistance you have with aligning your work schedule with the seasonal demands of your service industry. What will you do to resolve these?

14. Recall and describe the fears, resistances, or self-limiting patterns you experienced while completing this activity. What are you ready to do about them?

15. Reflect on the clarity you gained and describe how you feel empowered.

◆

The platespinner has an obvious relationship with balance—one plate too many and they start falling. One too few and he is distracted and feels out of sync. How many clients or projects can you balance with a feeling of control? At what limit does your life seem to crash?

Empowering Vision

Sample Work Scheduling Worksheet

		A	B	C	D	E	F
1	PROGRAM	Workshops	Intensives	Family Counseling	Group Counseling	Total $	Total hrs
2	January				x 3,200	3,200	40
3	February				x 3,200	3,200	40
4	March		x 7,200	x 960		8,160	104
5	April	x 3,200		x 960		4,160	56
6	May						
7	June				x 3,200	3,200	40
8	July				x 3,200	3,200	40
9	August	x 3,200				3,200	32
10	September		x 7,200			7,200	80
11	October			x 960	x 3,200	4,160	64
12	November			x 960	x 3,200	4,160	64
13	December	x 3,200		x 960		4,160	56
14	Annual Program Income	9,600	14,400	4,800	19,200	48,000	616
15	% of Total Annual Income	20%	30%	10%	40%		

© Empowering Vision

Work Scheduling Worksheet
Make copies of this form and use it as an original.

		A	B	C	D	E	F
1	PROGRAM					Total $	Total hrs
2	January						
3	February						
4	March						
5	April						
6	May						
7	June						
8	July						
9	August						
10	September						
11	October						
12	November						
13	December						
14	Annual Program Income						
15	% of Total Annual Income						

Empowering Vision

Additional Management Materials

Being in business is the process of asserting both your intentions and limits through your systems, policies and procedures. You do this by setting fees, offering discounts, and making agreements and simple contracts. You also do this by developing skill in collecting payments when they are due.

Fees, discounts, and collections are discussed in Activity 13; agreements and contracts in Activity 14. You may also review Appendix C, Checklist for Starting a Business, to determine if other managerial tools and activities are required for your business. Use Activity 15 to organize your filing system.

Fees, Discounts, and Collections

You create stability by setting fees, establishing a procedure to receive them, and collecting them when clients delay. Stability is also enhanced by knowing when to offer and accept discounts. Through simple policies and procedures, you can provide your service with ease and integrity.

> *"Cash flow management is essential
> to the success of every business.
> In fact, it is often more important
> that the ability to manufacture
> a product or generate a sale."*
>
> Bryan E. Milling

 ## Activity 13. Fees, Discounts, & Collections

1. **Fees.**

   a. To set your fees, begin by doing some research in your service industry. For each named program, determine and write in the chart on the next page the maximum, minimum, and average fees charged by others who offer the same or a similar service. Then add your current fee to the list. Within these parameters, determine how comfortable you are with your current fees.

   b. Add your preferred fees to the chart.

	Program	Minimum	Maximum	Average	Current	Preferred
1						
2						
3						
4						

    c. What are your reasons for choosing your current fee? If different, why do you not charge your preferred fee?

If you are still unclear about setting your fees, contact the Small Business Administration for a consultation with a SCORE (Senior Corps of Retired Executives) representative. This service is free, and the volunteers, who are all retired executives, can answer many of your questions about starting a new business.

Once you set your fee, be prepared to keep it for six months or a year. You can set different fees for different programs; consistency within each program is essential. If you plan to use a sliding fee scale, create a policy that clearly defines how the fee for each client is determined. Be consistent in following it.

As you set a fee, consider the possible consequences of raising it later:

- If you continually serve new clients, they will feel little impact from a fee increase unless they were referred by someone who told them your fees.

- If you serve repeat clientele almost exclusively, you may feel uncomfortable raising your fee. It may be best to set fees a little higher at the beginning.

- If fees are listed in your ads or promotional materials, these must be changed when your fees are raised. An alternative is to list them on an insert or to delete them from your materials altogether.

2. **Offering Discounts.**

The accounting system described in this manual is the cash system, which means that we have not included instructions in the Financial Matters section for regular invoicing. Based on this system, therefore, we assume you receive payment when you provide the service. However, it may be common in your service industry to invoice clients. If so, you will need to see your accountant or a simple accounting book for guidance on setting up an accrual accounting system with an accounts receivable journal and statements for each client.

Upon occasion you may need to invoice clients, however. A simple way to keep track of accounts receivable is to put all unpaid client invoices, alphabetically, in a folder marked

"Accounts Receivable" in alphabetical order. Check the folder monthly and follow up quickly on past-due payments. See Question 4 in this activity for information on preparing invoices. If you choose, you can offer clients discounts for prompt payment. However, first evaluate whether your net earnings are adequate to afford you the flexibility of offering discounts. Consider the points listed below.

- If you want to offer discounts, refer to Activity 27, Receipts Journal, Question 5, Page 136, to determine how to add a Discount Schedule to your accounting system. Your accountant will use the Discount Schedule to determine what portion of the discounts may be used to reduce your income for tax purposes.

- If your cash flow is strong and stable, you can afford to wait thirty days for payment. Offering a discount gives clients incentive to pay sooner. By giving up a small percentage of income, you encourage prompt payment. Consider whether you want the full amount later or slightly less now.

- The standard early payment discount is 2/10/Net 30. This entitles your client to subtract two percent from the total due if payment is made within ten days. If not, the total amount is due within thirty days.

- To increase your client base, you can also offer discounts during special promotions. (See Activity 20, Section C, Page 93.)

3. **Receiving Discounts.**

   If your creditors offer you a discount for early payment, consider: if your cash flow is strong, you can "earn" some money by receiving the discount. On the other hand, if your cash flow is weak, you can "borrow" your creditor's money for thirty days without paying interest.

4. **Invoicing and Collections.**

   a. You may feel uncomfortable about collecting money, but like sales, it is a necessary skill for success. You can minimize the need to collect from clients by stating your fees openly, receiving payment when services are rendered, and giving estimates (preferably in writing) for lengthy projects. If you are working on a lengthy or ongoing project, ask for a deposit of one-third of the fee in advance. Collect another third about half-way through the project and the rest when you submit the completed project.

   b. Written policies enhance clarity for everyone concerned. They also provide a structure so that your relationships can be mutually empowering. On each invoice type, have printed, or use a rubber stamp to print your policy. A typical payment policy reads:

Section 1. Management

> Invoices are payable upon receipt. Amounts unpaid after thirty days are subject to a service charge of 1.5 percent per month.

or

> Payment in full is due within thirty days. A $3.00 rebilling charge is added for payments made after the above date.

If you are tempted to leave the above phrase off an invoice because you believe the client will pay, reconsider. People are unpredictable, forgetful, and circumstances change. Protect your relationships and encourage integrity by stating your policies directly.

c. If you have not received payment within thirty days, follow up with a telephone call. Your client may have forgotten to pay and will send a check right away. Perhaps circumstances have changed, and he or she will indicate when a payment can be made. It's also possible that the payment was lost in the mail.

d. Also follow up overdue invoices with a statement recapping the unpaid invoice numbers, amounts, amount paid, and service charge. For Example: (See next page.)

Robert R. Johnson			135 Main Street • Anytown, CO 80999	
DATE	DESCRIPTION	CHARGES	PAYMENTS	BALANCE
8/15	Counseling	45.00		45.00
9/15	Counseling	45.00		90.00
9/30	Service charge	.68		90.68
10/15	Payment		45.00	45.68

or

Your Letterhead

10/31/91
TO: Client's Name
FOR: 3 hours word processing, 8/15/86

INVOICE DATE	INVOICE AMOUNT	AMOUNT PAID	SERVICE CHARGE	AMOUNT DUE
8/15/91	45.00			45.00
9/30/91		0.00	3.00	48.00
10/31/91		0.00	3.00	51.00

If payment is not received in thirty days, there is a $3.00 charge for each rebilling.

e. If you generally bill amounts under $50.00, you may want to include a minimum service charge to cover the time and expense of sending statements. Be sure to state this to your clients first.

f. Returned checks can be another cause for tension. It's important to create a clear policy and procedure in case you experience this. Always follow up on returned checks. The returned check may be the result of the client's oversight; telephone him or her to request a new check. You may want to add a returned check policy and fee. The accepted amount is $10-$25 per returned check. This must be printed or clearly stated.

In some circumstances, you may request a money order or cashier's check. For example, if a client is unorganized with his or her finances and subjects you to periodic returned checks, you may choose to request future payments in cash, cashier's checks, or money orders.

This is a sensitive issue in business. Follow your instincts and be willing to experiment until you find your own comfort level and guidelines.

g. If you choose, you can contract with a collection agency. These agencies relate directly with your client, file appropriate papers, go to court if necessary, absorb the expenses, and retain about half the amount they collect as your agent. An agency can also advise you on setting your policies.

5. **Paying Invoices.**

Many businesses pay invoices at the first and fifteenth of each month. When paying expenses, you may want to give priority to the following:

- Internal Revenue Service: The penalties and interest charged for late payment, and the anxiety that accompanies procrastination should place your IRS payments highest on your list. You may find it easier to open a business savings account and deposit 20 percent of each income deposit during a quarter, then file and pay taxes within two weeks of quarter's end. Thus federal, state, and self-employment tax payments are made with ease, and you earn interest.

- Adjunct services and/or suppliers: If you work with key people or businesses that are essential to your service and stability, pay them first.

- Rent, telephone and utility bills.

- If your expenses are greater than the cash in your account, make partial payments and include a note explaining the payment. Telephone your creditors to explain that you are unable to send a payment—no matter how uncomfortable or scared you are. To assure no interruption of service, let them know that you can't currently pay, but will pay by a specified date. This is far better than not communicating at all. Do not, from embarrassment or fear, indicate you will send more than you know you can. If you relate openly with creditors and suppliers, they will work with you. When you maintain the integrity with your creditors that you want from your clients, everyone thrives.

6. Reflect on the important points this activity revealed to you and describe how your management skills will be enhanced.

◆

Making Agreements and Contracts

This course is based on the belief that we are responsible for ourselves—for our success and for the consequences of our actions, intentions, and choices. Our thoughts, feelings, and beliefs about ourselves and the world shape the underlying attitudes and behavior we exhibit in our businesses. Every communication, interaction, and agreement is an extension of our beliefs, expectations, fears, and patterns. When we are honest, we can trust ourselves. When we trust ourselves, we experience the world as good and we enjoy our relationships and our businesses.

Yet, if we do not trust ourselves and interpret unexpected situations as problems, we may make—and then seek to justify—choices that lack integrity. The stability of our businesses can serve as a mirror. The choice is always ours, to live in honesty or be forever on the nervous edge.

When we agree to relationships with the intention of fulfilling only our own needs, there is little stability and integrity from which anyone can grow. In contrast, when we build a foundation from mutually honorable intentions, our relationships and agreements will reflect these, and everyone can thrive. This is seen in all relationships and, particularly, in business, where money becomes the symbol of our success with relationships.

Be clear about your objectives, expectations, and limits. Communicate them openly, and put them in writing as simple policies, procedures, and agreements. When you do, you establish a solid foundation for yourself as a professional.

As you clarify your policies, state them with new clients, create written agreements as appropriate, and follow through as agreed. If you choose to draw up a standard contract, we strongly suggest that you send a copy to your attorney for review. The legal fee will be well worth the peace of mind for everyone concerned.

Contracts. If you perform a standard service to all your clients with details and steps that need to be clearly outlined, a contract may serve your purposes. Your contract should clearly and concisely outline your objectives. Review your objectives and talk with your mentor or attorney for clarity.

Letter of Agreement. If your terms are simple or they vary with each client, they can be outlined in a short agreement for you and your client to sign and date.

If you determine that you must change your agreement, communicate immediately with your client and renegotiate. Likewise, if a client does not follow through as agreed, communicate with him or her immediately and create a new agreement. Make notes of the discussion and follow up with a letter confirming your agreements. Include an additional copy of the letter so that your client can sign and date it and you can each keep a copy.

"Communication always leads to transformation and growth."
Stan Hartman

Section 1. Management

Activity 14. Agreements & Contracts

Following is a list of the basic expectations and types of negotiation that require verbal and written definition. Both the contract and letter of agreement should contain as many of these points as are required for your specific circumstances. See the Sample Contract that follows for guidelines.

1. Begin by writing your objectives for a contract or agreement. This will help you build the foundation you want with your clients.

2. Explain the length, duration, number of hours and sessions, and frequency of your service program.

3. Include cost, payment terms, deposit, retainer fee, service charges, returned check fees, and other payment arrangements, as appropriate.

4. Include a cancellation notice and any charges for failure to provide notice. Define the conditions under which you will make exceptions to this policy.

5. State your insurance coverage, if applicable.

6. Include a confidentiality agreement, if appropriate.

7. Include the actions and level of commitment that you require from your client.

8. Include both the circumstances under which the contract may be terminated and the procedure for doing so.

9. Reflect on the important points this activity revealed to you and describe how your management skills will be enhanced.

Note: The guidelines offered here are written specifically to support you in creating a clear, mutually agreed upon relationship with your clients. Use this as a guide with all your other professional relationships as well.

◆

*"Every decision you make stems from what you think you are,
and represents the value that you put upon yourself."*
Accept This Gift

Sample Contract

PAYMENT CONTRACT

I agree to make payments totalling $330 for the *Empowering Vision* Course. In addition, I agree to pay service charges of $10 per month.

I agree to make payments as follows, under Plan A (4 payments, $20 service charge) or Plan B (2 payments, $10 service charge):

Plan A (4 payments, which include $20 service charge)

☐
- Nonrefundable deposit at registration — $100
- Payment by 4th class (week of October 19) — 85
- Payment by 7th class (week of November 9) — 85
- Final payment by last class (week of November 30) — 80
- Total — $350

Plan B: (2 payments, which include $10 service charge)

☐
- Nonrefundable deposit at registration — $100
- Remainder by 4th class (week of October 19) — 240
- Total — $340

I understand that my attendance at the first class commits me to this payment schedule.

Payment Policies:
- Payments must be current to insure continuing admission to class.
- Payments are due before the 4th, 7th or last class begins, whether mailed or brought to class. Make checks payable to *Empowering Vision* and mail to Empowering Vision, P.O. Box 18296, Boulder, CO 80308-8296.
- Early payments may be made to reduce service charge.
- A $25 service charge will be added for any check returned by the bank for any reason.

_____
Participant's Signature

Please keep a copy of this agreement for your records.

Organizing Your Paperwork

To ensure your chances for success, create a filing system for your support documents and records—all paperwork that you give out and collect in your business negotiations and transactions. Easy access to these documents helps you manage your business and use your time effectively.

In addition, by law, you are required to retain all financial records regarding expenses, deductions and income for three years after the date of your tax return. IRS Publications #583, Information for Business Tax Preparers, and #334, Small Business Tax Guide, contain further information on record keeping and record retention requirements.

Obviously, it is important to be well organized. Think of your business as a Rolls Royce engine—one that runs so smoothly and quietly that you don't hear it. Organization will keep your business in that kind of running order. The following guidelines will help you create the filing system that will best support you.

Activity 15. Filing System

1. **Filing System Materials.** This filing system is designed for a cabinet or box. You will need the following materials to set up your filing system (approximate prices are indicated):

    a. **A file container.** Choose your file container and system based on the amount of paper you will store and your budget. Begin simply; you can upgrade as needed. Options include standard metal office filing cabinets (two or four drawers, letter- or legal-sized, new or used, $50-$200); metal discount store cabinets (two or four drawers, letter-sized, $15-$25); cardboard boxes designed for use as file cabinets (available from discount and office supply stores, $4-$10). Letter-sized are usually adequate.

    b. **File folders** ($8-$15/100). Choose letter-sized (for 8-1/2"x11" papers) or legal-sized (for 8-1/2"x14" papers). The most convenient are 1/3-cut folders (the three tabs across alternate left, center, and right).

    c. **Hanging folders** (optional; $8-$10/25). These hang on a frame and keep your file drawers neater by providing more classification, and preventing files from slipping under others and becoming lost from view.

    d. **Hanging folder frames** (necessary only if you have hanging folders; $3 each). Some file cabinets come with built-in frames.

Empowering Vision

    e. **File folder labels** (optional; $3/box of 248). You can extend the life of a file folder by placing a new label over an old one. Typing the labels keeps files neater and easier to use. Or, if you want to reuse them, use pencil.

    f. **File Guides.** With hanging files, file guides are plastic tabs with paper inserts ($2.50/25) that may be attached to the hanging folders to indicate broad categories. Without hanging files, you may want blank or labeled A-Z file guides, to separate the file folders within a drawer ($35/100).

2. **Filing System.** Make your system simple and logical. Use the fewest number of sections and folders to begin, and add more when they are needed.

    a. Begin by listing the major business functions (Management, Program Planning & Development, Marketing, Public Relations, Accounting.) Each will be a major section in your filing system and will require a file guide.

    b. Think of the current level of activity in each of the above function/sections. How full do you think each section will be? Do you need to divide any of them into more detail? For example, Program Planning, Program Development, and Client Files may each require a section. Management may be divided into Planning, Administrative, and Accounting. The level of detail you need depends on the complexity of your business and the volume of your paperwork. Make a file guide for each section.

    c. Divide each major section into smaller categories for individual files. Will you need a separate file for each client, will one be sufficient for each program's clients, or will you need a file for all the A's, the B's, the C's, or perhaps A-G, H-N, O-Z? Do you have enough correspondence to warrant monthly files (Correspondence - June, 1991) or subject files (Correspondence with AMA)? Or do you write so few letters that one file labeled Correspondence - 1991 will be adequate? Look over Activity 25, Chart of Accounts, to determine what files you will need for your Income and Expense categories. Begin simply; if a file becomes too full, you can subdivide it later.

    d. Create a label for each smaller category you indicated. Include the major category and smaller category, as appropriate. Affix the label to the folder. For example:

> **RECEIPTS**
> Travel and Entertainment
>
> Market Research
>
> **Administration**
> CLIENT CONTRACTS

Section 1. Management

    e. If possible, put each piece of paper—letter, invoice, market research notes, planning outlines, contracts—into the proper file when you are finished with it. File papers in chronological order, with the oldest material at the back. Keep everything in the same direction and fold oversized pages neatly.

    f. If you prefer, create a container called "Filing," and take a few minutes each week to file papers before they accumulate. You can file papers during telephone conversations that require little concentration or while you are on "hold."

3. However you organize your filing system, use our suggestions to guide you to create the system for your unique way of thinking. The point is for it to serve you. Enjoy creating it so that it does.

◆

Anxiety and chaos...

transform to ease with effective systems.

61

Marketing

Introduction

As you complete the activities in this section, you will determine who is ready to buy your service and develop a marketing strategy. In this step-by-step process, you will determine the activities through which you will utilize your available resources—time, energy, money, and people—to promote your service.

"Nothing is difficult that is wholly desired"
Accept This Gift

If your service is new, or if it is a revolutionary twist on an old idea, or if you are promoting your service to a market segment that has not yet expressed a demand for it, you may discover that you need to educate potential clients. You may also discover that you need to educate yourself about your clients. Clearly, if you know all about them—their attitudes, beliefs, preferences, and level of sophistication—you can be straightforward about how your service will enhance their lives. Through your understanding, exhibited on your promotional materials and in conversation, potential clients, in turn, will acquire enough information to decide whether they want the benefits your service offers.

Market Research

As you begin determining how to promote your service, it is essential to conduct market research. The objectives are to:

- Know your target clientele
- Become knowledgeable about your competition
- Determine the maturity level and health of your service industry in the geographical area you choose to serve.

As you progress through the marketing activities, you will want to conduct market research to answer the questions that will naturally arise. Use the following suggestions as needed.

1. To learn about your service industry, take successful persons with similar services (not in your geographical service area) to lunch, afternoon tea, or for a drink. Discuss your ideas and concerns, and listen to their opinions and perspectives. Find out what they have done that has and has not been effective. Take notes. Collect their promotional materials.

2. Meet with direct competitors to discuss your mutual service industry, how your services are different or similar, what works and what doesn't, and the ways you can be mutually supportive. If appropriate, experience your competitor's service and invite him/her to experience yours. (Exchange checks for accounting and tax purposes.) Exchange promotional materials.

3. Have lunch, tea, or a drink with someone who offers a similar service but who does not serve the same clientele. Discuss, share, and find ways to be supportive or make referrals. Exchange promotional materials.

4. Meet with people who know and value your service to hear their perspective on your ideas and concerns. Their opinions and support can be invaluable.

5. Listen to ideas and perspectives from people who know very little about your service. In their naiveté, they can add valuable information to your research.

6. Ask the reference librarian to help you find articles and research studies on your topic. Both public and university libraries are useful.

7. Look in the Yellow Pages and service directories for similar services, competitors, new clients, and so forth.

8. Read trade journals and periodicals related to your industry. Clip newspaper articles and keep research files on topics of interest to you.

9. Attend your industry's conventions, exhibits, fairs, or trade shows. Collect information and make contacts.

10. Give yourself an hour session with a marketing consultant or mentor to review your promotion plan (from Activity 21). Perhaps you can trade your services for the consultant's time. (Exchange checks for accounting and tax purposes.)

11. The marketing consultant or mentor can also help you create a questionnaire to survey potential clients on their needs, desires, and buying patterns.

12. Be aware of the many valuable contacts and bits of information you come across that can help you provide an even better service. Save these in a file and keep a note pad with you.

13. Add to this list any new ways you think of or hear about that can help you learn what you need.

… Section 2. Marketing

An Overview of the Marketing Strategy

The marketing strategy for each program depends upon your vision, goals, careful organization of your time, and marketing budget. With those clearly established, you can utilize what your market research tells you about your competition and your own position within the marketplace to evaluate possible promotional campaigns (advertising, direct sales, sales promotions, networking, publicity). Keeping in mind what you have learned about the behavior of your targeted clientele, you can design the promotion plan that will best utilize your resources.

A different strategy may be required for each of your income-generating programs. The strategy will depend on the specific application of your service, the client profile, and the mix of promotional campaigns and materials you choose. Taking the time to create a careful marketing strategy will maximize your exposure and help you build a full clientele.

To create your marketing strategy, follow these steps for each of your programs:

1. Be clear about your intention—your vision and specific goals (from Activity 2, Current Vision).

2. Describe your service, the quality you want to offer, and your business image (Activity 9, Your Service, Quality, & Image).

3. Develop your service into appropriate income-generating programs and create an outline for each. Select one as the focus of your promotional materials and promotion plan (from Activities 10 and 11, Narrowing Your Focus and Program Planning and Development, respectively. Use Activity 12 to Project Your Ideal Workload).

4. Conduct the necessary market research. (See Market Research, Page 63.)

5. Identify your clientele and develop a client profile for your programs. (Complete Activity 16, Client Profile.)

6. Determine others who serve your clientele. (Activity 17, Competition.)

7. Evaluate your service industry's growth stage within your service area. (Activity 18, Your Service Industry's Growth Stage.)

8. Determine the right positioning objectives, slogan, and messages. (Activity 19, Positioning Objectives & Messages.)

9. Develop promotional materials. (Activity 24, Planning Promotional Materials.)

10. Evaluate possible campaigns. (Activity 20, Promotional Campaigns.)

11. Get strong endorsements from high visibility clients. (Activity 20, B1, Page 92.)

12. Develop your promotional campaigns. (Activity 20, Promotional Campaigns.)

13. Create a promotion plan. (Activity 21, Promotion Plan.)

14. Prepare sales support tools. (Activities 22, Direct Sales. and 23, Cover Letter, respectively.)

15. As needed, add tasks and activities to your time management plans. (Activities 6-8 on time management.)

16. Add activities to your appointment book, when appropriate.

17. Carry out your plan, adjusting your CPM Chart, appointment book, and plan as needed.

18. Conduct additional market research as needed. The more information you collect, the more knowledgeable you become about your industry, the market, and your own special niche. The more you know, the more you empower yourself.

Once you have created a plan that you are comfortable with, follow it for a few months and evaluate it periodically to revise the portions that are obsolete or that do not provide the return you want. Perhaps you will decide on a new approach altogether. As the the seasons change, and as your clientele changes, you will want to change your marketing strategy. You will adapt it to increased and decreased competition and to increased and decreased demand as well.

Before you begin any promotional effort, make sure there really is a need for your service in the geographical area you are considering. Make sure your timing for change is right and that you are ready for the demands of change. Do you have the support you want to make the transition gracefully? Planning your promotions wisely will allow you to act with intent rather than react.

"Anything that is made by force meets its end in a like manner."
Carl Sherrell

Targeting Your Clients

Marketing success depends on your ability to match your service with the segment of society that is ready to buy. The following activity is designed to help you identify these people by describing them in the demographic and psychographic terms explained below. Your success will increase as you begin to know your potential clients, in terms of your service, almost better than they know themselves. Only then can you create promotional materials that truly speak to them.

To begin, sit quietly for a moment, get comfortable, and close your eyes. As you relax, think of your service, and remember why it's important to you.

Now, reflect on the people you think are ready for your service. Describe them to yourself. What are they like? What are their values and standards? Where are they? What are they doing? Why are they doing this? Why do you think they live their lives as they do? What motivates them?

Now you have an idea of who is ready to buy your service. Complete this activity to learn even more about your clients, their needs, and preferences.

Activity 16. Client Profile

1. Read the following a) demographic, b) psychographic, and c) lifestyle descriptions to evaluate the qualities that describe your target clientele.

    a. **Demographics** provide the general ways of evaluating people and sorting them into broad categories. Demographic characteristics include: race, sex, religion, age, marital status, occupation, income, degrees and credentials, education and training, family size, parenting situation, sexual preference, impairments, and urban/suburban/rural location.

    b. **Psychographics** differentiate people by describing various lifestyles and preferences. Psychographics include: personal patterns, desires, beliefs, values, consumer choices, and lifestyle needs. For example, we are not only female, white, middle-aged, non-smokers; we eat sprouts, tofu, and drink an occasional glass of wine.

    c. **Lifestyle evaluation** provides the information that differentiates people as unique, yet still similar to others. Used with psychographic information, lifestyle considerations* include the following:

These items are from Stanford Research Institute's International Values and Lifestyles Program, Summary of Report No. 18, February 1981.

Active and spectator sports	Cigarette smoking
Bowling, pool, and billiards	Self-learning
Chess and backgammon	Pleasure or business travel
Outdoor activities	Shopping habits
The arts, cultural events, movies	Ownership and use of credit cards
Youth entertainments	Having life and health insurance
The inner life	TV watching and preferences
Poker or bridge	Radio listening
Gardening or baking	Newspaper or magazine reading
Needlework	Housing
Eating habits, including eating out and health-related food concerns	Working at home
	Using libraries

2. Determine who is ready for your service by answering the following questions:

   a. With the detail appropriate for your service from Question 1, describe your typical clients. Include information about their personal and professional lifestyles, as appropriate. Describe the reasons for their choices.

   b. How do you think your target clientele regards your service? Include any beliefs or opinions—positive or negative—that you think strongly influence their attitudes. Describe how you are ready to address them.

   c. Explain why your target clientele is ready for your service.

   d. What, specifically, do you think these clients want from you? Why? Include how you think your specialty and quality fit their needs, preferences, and standards.

   e. Explain how your image and style fit their needs and preferences.

   f. Will your clients come to you, or will you go to them? What distances are involved? Evaluate your comfort level with this arrangement and make any needed changes.

   g. Determine the potential size of this market. Is it broad enough to fulfill your income goals? If not, what will you do?

   h. What days and hours will clients use your service?

   i. Determine the fee range—the upper and lower limits—these clients will pay for your service.

   j. What other client information do you need?

3. Describe any attitudes, beliefs, and biases that you hold that might interfere with a mutually satisfying relationship with these people. Evaluate these and determine what you are ready to do to release them.

Section 2. Marketing

4. Determine your level of confidence in your ability to communicate your thoughts and feelings to them, especially in difficult circumstances. Describe any changes you want to make.

5. Describe the personal satisfaction you gain from serving these clients.

6. Describe the fears, resistances, or self-limiting patterns you experienced while completing this activity. What are you ready to do about them?

7. Reflect on the clarity you gained during this activity and describe how you feel empowered. Explain how this will affect your ability to reach and attract the clients who are ready for your service.

8. What must you learn and what skills must you develop to better serve your clients? What resources will you draw upon? List the steps you will take and include dates, when appropriate.

◆

Marketing success depends on your ability to match your service with the segment of society that is ready to buy.

Analyzing Your Competition

Empowering Vision is based on the belief that the key to success is in knowing yourself, your needs, desires, strengths, resources, limits, and boundaries. Next, know your target clientele a bit better than they know themselves. Finally, know what your competition offers. As colleagues, create a relationship, be mutually supportive, perhaps even refer to each other or combine your skills in a new project or service.

Your competition consists of the people in the same kind of business and industry. Found together in the Yellow Pages, you are not just competing with each other for would-be clients. You can also inspire one another and seek new ways to improve and uplift your industry. By doing this, you can enhance the shared quality of life.

"Competitors" fulfill a social need that has been identified by a large or small segment of society. Perhaps they also fulfill an evolutionary need that, when satisfied, will promote excellence, quality, and integrity.

Many people are uncomfortable when they hear the word "competition," and some even feel fearful. Self-limiting patterns—fear of failure, fear of inadequacy, lack of self-trust—all suppress our natural instinct to experience ourselves as part of a larger context in which we all fulfill our needs together.

Knowing your competition or, at least, knowing about them—their specialties, strengths, and limitations—and knowing how their services compare with and complement yours, builds confidence. In knowing your market position and theirs, you take your place and fulfill your unique function. This is done not by competing, but through the strength, vitality, and quality you offer.

Remember to view your competition through the eyes of your clients. It is from their perspective that you identify your competition. For most service areas there are three categories of competition:

- Experts—those respected, successful professionals who probably earn top dollar
- Colleagues—those who offer the same quality, service, and specialty as you
- Newcomers—those who are just starting their businesses.

Collect their brochures, read their ads, clip their newspaper and magazine articles. As you learn about them, you will see your position, your uniqueness, as well as what you have in common with your competitors. This information will help you with marketing decisions. When you request information, do so in an open, friendly tone, explaining who you are, what you do, and that you would like information. Explain that you offer a similar service and that you are doing some market research. You can offer to meet, get to know one another, and discuss how you can be supportive.

Knowing your competition can benefit everyone. Someone who does not really fit your client profile will appreciate an honest acknowledgement that, "I don't do the type of work you are requesting, but I suggest you call…" Competition can bring forth the best in everyone.

Activity 17. Competition

Note: Some of the following questions require market research. See Pages 63 and 64 for ideas.

1. **Competitors.** List your immediate competitors within your client service area. Include their fees. For assistance, look in the Yellow Pages, newspapers, service directories, networking bulletin boards, and ask others. Evaluate these to determine whether they would be regarded by your target clientele as experts or your colleagues. Next to each name, write "Expert" or "Colleague." If you are not sure, ask several clients for their opinion.

2. **Experts.** From Question 1, list each expert—competitors who are well known and respected—including those outside your service area who might still attract your clientele. Collect and read their promotional materials. After you have read your competitors' brochures, answer the following questions for each. If appropriate, you can group your competitors and answer the questions accordingly. Remember to consider your answers from the perspective of your target clientele, unless otherwise stated.

    a. What specific clientele do they serve?

    b. Describe their programs, benefits, unique qualities, and fees.

    c. What image do they project?

    d. Evaluate whether they maintain a high profile, how they have become known, how long they have been established, and how they currently attract clients.

    e. What do these services provide that you do not? Describe their competitive advantages, if any.

    f. Explain why your clients regard these competitors as experts and why they would pay top dollar for their services.

    g. If your responses to a-f are incomplete, or if you are unclear about your clients' viewpoint, consider preparing a survey of a few questions to obtain the necessary information. Give it to a varied sampling of your potential clients. Refer to Market Research (Page 63) for other ideas on researching your service industry.

    h. Have you received their service? If yes, describe what you received. If no, determine the circumstances under which you would use their services.

    i. Record your thoughts and feelings about their services. How do you regard them?

    j. In what ways do they inspire excellence in you?

    k. Do you choose to reach their level of expertise? If yes, how will you?

l. How would you like to develop mutually supportive relationships, make referrals, or affiliate together?

m. In general, what are your thoughts and feelings as you answer these questions? What do you want to do about these, if anything?

3. **Colleagues and Newcomers.** List separately or in groups, your equals within your service area. Evaluate their services and answer the appropriate questions from 2a-m.

4. **You** (insert your business name here). In this section, determine how you believe your service compares with your competition and is regarded by your target clientele and by others in your service industry. As with Questions 2 and 3, use a-m as your guide, and do only the questions that apply.

5. What is your specialty and position in your client service area?

6. In terms of your specialty, how do you think your target clients regard your business? How do they regard you?

7. Summarize your competitive advantages. What new ones can you develop? Which ones will you develop at this time?

8. If the way you regard your service differs from the way your clientele regards your service, explain the differences. What will you do as a result?

9. Ask eight to ten of your clients Question 2e, in regard to your service.

10. Describe the fears, resistances, or self-limiting patterns that you experienced while completing this activity. What are you ready to do about them?

11. Reflect on the important points in this activity and describe how you feel empowered. How will this affect the stability of your business?

12. As you reflect on your experience while completing this activity, what must you learn and develop? What resources are you ready to draw on? List the steps you will take and include dates, when appropriate.

◆

Section 2. Marketing

Evaluating Your Service Industry

Now that you have identified your clientele and competitors, you will evaluate the service industry of which your business is a part. The vitality and productivity of your service industry depends on the current demand for the service, the number of competitors, their levels of quality, and the unique contribution each makes. In essence, society's demand for your service, along with current economic conditions, creates the stage of a service industry's growth and development.

> "The conscious choice, in my mind,
> is the commitment to life;
> not my life, but Life."
> John Denver

Because they satisfy society's changing needs and desires, most industries develop, evolve, and die as do people and cultures. Industries that satisfy basic needs—food, communication, or health care—endure regardless of changes in society. Their forms and legal requirements change according to evolving needs and desires. Industries that serve short-term needs or passing desires die or become outdated when society seeks to satisfy its needs elsewhere.

The Infancy Stage

Competitors begin businesses in response to demand. If the need is great, an industry can develop rapidly through the first few stages. Remember the initial excitement that accompanied the introduction of copy shops, hot tub spas, and video rental stores.

Knowing your industry's growth stage gives you information you can use to fine tune your marketing strategy. You will also be better prepared for the challenges presented by your industry's changes.

The five growth stages—beginning with infancy and progressing to late maturity—are similar to the stages of human development. As you read through the following, determine the stage that best describes your industry in your client service area.

At an industry's birth and during its **infancy**, most people haven't yet recognized the need or desire the industry satisfies. A few people may have identified the need or desire and would use the service if they knew about it. A few others may have read or heard about the service and are curious about what the leading edge offers. They'll be among the first to use this service. Because of the relatively low number of initial clients, people in the earliest businesses must create momentum through education. The personal computer industry provides a good example of successful infancy stage activity. In the early 1980s, the general public rarely thought about personal computers. Few people understood their capacity. Now, the millions who own personal computers cannot imagine how they managed without them.

In the **growth** stage, the public has begun to experience the need or desire that the emerging industry satisfies. At this stage, businesses enter the industry at a rapid rate. An example is desktop publishing, an offspring of the personal computer industry that was unheard of until the mid-1980s. During the growth stage, businesses come and go quickly. Many of these business are started and operated without adequate planning, management, or capital.

The Growth Stage

The number of businesses an industry can support depends on the strength of the need/desire and the corresponding number of buyers. If there are more businesses than needed, **a shakeout** occurs, for a variety of reasons. Perhaps too many businesses are trying to satisfy the need (i.e., computers); a social issue causes an abrupt change in consumer behavior (e.g., the emergence of herpes and AIDS affected the use of hot tub spas); or the public's taste suddenly changes (e.g., when the urban cowboy craze ended abruptly, many western wear manufacturers lost their shirts). Businesses that are inadequately capitalized, poorly managed, and ineffectively marketed will fail. The computer industry provides many examples. Osborne and Otrona, early entrants in the market, were displaced as soon as IBM caught up.

The Shakeout Stage

After a shakeout, an industry—like any other dynamic system—will begin to stabilize. As the remaining businesses are managed through change, the industry scales down to meet demand. At this point, the industry enters its **maturity** stage. It has become a household word and its service becomes a stable component of society.

In the **late maturity** stage, an industry is supported by a few loyalists. Drive-in theaters are an example of a need becoming extinct, especially in suburban areas, where land has grown too valuable for low-income use. Occasionally, some of these businesses can profit from little or no competition. People nostalgic for the products of another era may try—and like—old services. In

Section 2. Marketing

The Maturity Stage

this way, some outdated industries are kept alive. A new fad can also bring new life to a traditional industry. (Witness the preppy look that gave new popularity to classic clothing styles.) Nonetheless, client choices will always be based on the satisfaction of personal needs and desires.

Frequently the satisfaction of one need creates a new demand and a new industry. Consider, for example, the evolution of the adding machine to the calculator, which in turn led to computers. It often makes good business sense to focus on satisfying the next level of need. Some of the most successful businesses like to stay at the leading edge and create new services and industries. A new fad can also give new life to a traditional industry.

As you read through the next activity, consider the general public's awareness of the need or desire that your service industry satisfies. Considering all the demands on their daily attention, time, and money, how necessary is this need or desire to them? If it is essential, new, or exciting, people will want to use your service.

The Late-Maturity Stage

If you understand your service industry's role in satisfying both basic and changing needs, you will be able to adapt effectively to changes in society, and in your community. If you have neither the time nor the inclination to keep abreast of your industry's developments and economic changes, you will want to call on the knowledge, wisdom, and support of your mentors. Or, you may choose to contract with an advisor or hire a business manager, even on a part-time basis. Remember, however, that you will need an understanding of these concepts to choose someone you can trust.

In Activity 18, remember that in these rapidly changing times, circumstances are evolving and factors are changing even as you answer these questions. Determine whether your industry is at the beginning, middle, or end of the stage in your service area. Remember, an industry's maturity level can vary from region to region. Be aware of changes in your industry and manage your business accordingly.

Empowering Vision

✍ Activity 18. Your Service Industry's Growth Stage

Note: If you need help answering any of these questions, ask your mentor or refer to Market Research, Pages 63 and 64, for ways to assess your industry. Complete this activity for each of your programs, if appropriate.

1. Name your service industry. If you are unsure, think about where it would be listed in the Yellow Pages, or in a catalogue of services. Write a brief description of your service industry.

2. Explain the basic need or desire that your service industry fulfills in society. Why does this need exist? Explain how the fulfillment of this need or desire enhances the quality of life.

3. If applicable, explain the evolutionary need (see Glossary) your service industry fulfills. What is your service industry contributing during this time of great personal and global change?

4. Review Activity 9, Service, Quality, & Image. Review Activity 17, Competition. Describe your specialization in the context of your industry.

5. Read the following descriptions of the stages of growth, first from your own perspective, then from the perspective of your target clientele. Choose the stage that applies to your industry in your client service area. Explain your choice. Then, answer the questions following the stage you select. (If you need help choosing a growth stage, consult others.)

    a. **Infancy Stage:** Since you are offering a new service or perhaps adding a revolutionary twist to an old one, you will need to create a demand for your service. Few people acknowledge or understand the need or desire that your service satisfies. Most are uninformed and many are skeptical. By educating people, you will help them move beyond their resistance and try your service at least once.

    Your personal challenges will be handling rejection and being patient with your progress as you educate people. You will need to explain your service in terms that stimulate your target clientele. You must help them identify and experience the need or desire your service satisfies, then help them decide if they want to choose your service over others. Through assertiveness and gentle perseverance, you will overcome your fear of rejection and you will learn patience with others' resistance.

    1) Explain your comfort level with assertiveness and with active promoting.

    2) Explain your confidence in your service and in your ability to present it easily.

    3) Describe your patience level when you feel you are making little progress.

    4) Describe your ability to handle resistance and rejection.

    5) Describe your verbal and written communication skills.

6) How long do you estimate your service industry will remain at its current stage of development in your service area? What will shift it to the next level? Explain your reasoning.

7) If you experienced discomfort while answering these questions, explain what you felt and why. Describe any fear, resistance, or limitation you are now experiencing. Explain what you will do to address these issues.

b. **Growth Stage:** In this stage, you will notice that new businesses are emerging at a rapid rate. More potential clients are available, and they are increasingly knowledgeable and enthusiastic about your service.

Your personal challenges may be with the issues of competition, the fear of being left out, insecurity, jealousy, and feelings of inadequacy. You will need to feel strong, centered, and confident about your special qualities.

1) How do you honestly feel about competition?

2) Describe what you automatically do when you feel insecure, left out, jealous, or inadequate. Determine the effect of this pattern.

3) How long do you estimate your service industry will remain at its current level of development in your service area? What might shift it to the next level? Explain your reasoning.

4) If you experienced discomfort while answering these questions, explain what you felt and why. Describe any feelings of fear, resistance, or limitation you are now experiencing.

5) Explain the attitude changes and actions necessary to address these issues and empower yourself.

c. **Shakeout Stage:** Your industry has been rapidly accepted, and many more businesses exist than the market can support. Many of these businesses are inadequately capitalized and managed. Marketing, planning, and other skills are lacking. Or, perhaps an unexpected social issue or change has threatened the entire industry. Many businesses in the industry are failing. You may feel as though the bottom is falling out, and, indeed, it may be!

Your personal challenge is to manage your feelings, yourself, and your business during a challenging time. You may, at times, feel as though you are on an emotional merry-go-round. The ability to manage your feelings, especially fear, is the true key to success, so evaluate and sort through the many feelings you experience. In addition, you will want to be calm with your clients and provide an even better service so they will continue to work with you during this challenging period. Stability is the bottom line. With self-acceptance, faith, focus, and skill, you

Empowering Vision

will manage your business better than you imagined. After your industry begins to stabilize, your business will begin to grow again. Eventually, it will stabilize.

1) List and describe limitations in your business that might weaken its stability during a challenging time.

2) How do you typically handle your feelings of instability? Explain how you react during crisis.

3) Describe typical feelings of fear or insecurity; include the self-limiting patterns you know will affect your stability and reliability. Explain the actions you will take to address these patterns and empower yourself.

4) How long do you estimate your service industry will remain at its current stage of development within your service area? What might shift it to the next level? Explain your reasoning.

5) List and describe the resources you know are available for support. How will you receive this support?

6) Describe how you can better serve your clients and utilize their referrals to maintain stability through this time.

d. **Maturity Stage:** After the shakeout, services that still satisfy a need or desire for some segment of society will stabilize. The remaining businesses will create a healthy, competitive environment. Tension and strife will be reduced, and everything may seem relatively easy. If your goals are simple, or if you are satisfied with "getting-by," you can manage with little effort.

Your personal challenge will be to rise above complacency, procrastination, administrative disorganization, and marketing passivity.

1) Describe any tendencies you have toward complacency, procrastination, disorganization, and passivity. One at a time, explain how you think these traits will inhibit the growth and stability of your business.

2) Describe what you are ready to do to address these traits so that your business will thrive.

3) How long do you estimate your service industry will remain at its current level of development in your service area? What might shift it to the next level? Explain your reasoning.

e. **Late Maturity Stage:** Having served its purpose or having been changed by a social issue, the need your industry satisfies has declined or has evolved to a different level. Your clients are satisfying that need with a different service, and

Section 2. Marketing

growth in your industry has slowed or become stagnant. Your industry may require stimulation—perhaps through broader acceptability, visibility, and exposure; or by adding a new service or developing a new approach to an old service. Maybe the industry will simply become extinct. At this stage, you will notice that business is dropping off, although you still have a few loyal clients.

Your personal challenge is to accept change, and maybe even to create it. With vision, ingenuity, and perseverance, your challenge is to create a strategy that will either profitably re-establish your service or create a new one. Begin with some market research. Call several former clients to ask why they no longer use your service and what they have chosen instead.

1) Explain how you typically feel and act when change forces you to be flexible and make new choices. Explain how these patterns affect you. Evaluate which are supportive, which are not, and what you are ready to do to empower yourself.

2) Determine whether you have enough remaining loyal clients to provide the income you need. Do you want to continue serving this select few? Explain your reasoning.

3) How long do you estimate your service industry will remain at its current level of development in your service area? What might shift it to the next level? Explain your reasoning.

4) Determine whether you choose to create a new approach, based on the old, or change to something completely new. Explain your reasoning.

5) Describe your new service in detail (See Activity 9, Service, Quality, & Image, and Activity 11, Program Planning & Development). Then, identify the growth stage of its service industry. Complete Activity 16, Client Profile, and Activity 17, Competition.

6. Describe the fears, resistances, or self-limiting patterns you experienced while completing this activity. What are you ready to do about them?

7. Reflect on the important points in this activity and describe how you feel empowered. How will this affect your ability to reach and attract the clients you choose?

8. What must you learn and develop? What resources are you ready to draw upon? List the steps you will take and include dates, when appropriate.

◆

Positioning and Communication

Now that you have evaluated your industry, it is time to take your position among your competitors, and communicate to your target clientele. You will need to solidify the information you have compiled into a succinct message and plan of action. The next three activities will help you organize the right promotion plan, one that makes efficient and effective use of your time, energy, and other resources.

These activities will help you:

- Determine your positioning objective and message slant (Activity 19)

- Evaluate the many ways you can promote your service, and select the right one(s) for you now (Activity 20)

- Systematically plan each promotional campaign and create a complete promotion plan by combining all your campaigns (Activity 21).

The objective of your promotion plan is to inform potential clients that your business exists and, even more importantly, that your business will best serve their needs. This is accomplished with a promotion plan (Activity 21), a sales presentation (Activity 22), and promotional materials (Activity 24).

Positioning is the process by which you establish yourself in the minds of your target clients. You want your clients to think of your business whenever they need your service. For example, you may think of IBM when you hear "computers," Xerox when you hear "copiers," McDonald's when you hear "hamburgers." These three companies have firmly positioned themselves as the leaders in their industries.

To position yourself, find a niche and utilize your uniqueness to establish yourself firmly in that niche. For example, your position can revolve around price or quality: "The most expensive (or the best) exercise studio in town." Or, it can revolve around special scheduling: "Enjoy a massage after 7 p.m." Or you can create a new twist on a recognized concept, as 7-Up did with its "Uncola" campaign.

When you are the first to offer a new service or one with a unique slant, you generally make a lasting impression with clients. People tend to remember the first to do something. Through quality and consistency, you will remain solidly in their minds.

Positioning is accomplished through your own willingness to analyze your competition and your industry, and then reach your clientele through a strong promotion campaign. (Campaign options are described in Activity 20.) Once you choose a position, you can establish and maintain yourself in it by projecting a strong, consistent image and by providing a quality service.

The first step is to position your business in the minds of your target clientele. By using your positioning objective, name, positioning slogan, positioning messages, promotional materials, sales presentations, time, energy, money, people, and perseverance, you will create a plan that is right for you.

Activity 19, Positioning Objectives & Messages, will help you position your business within your client service area in several ways. You will begin by determining your positioning objective. You will choose the business name and positioning slogan that describes your unique position in your service area. Finally, your basic positioning message will tell your clients exactly what you do. Then, they can determine if they are ready to contact you.

This activity will help you create your promotional materials, including your business cards and letterhead, brochures, flyers, advertising copy, and sales presentation. Because the colors, type style, and paper you choose create an image and make strong statements about your service, use Activity 24, Planning Promotional Materials, to help you blend these elements into an effective visual presentation.

> *"Fine art is that in which the hand,
> the head, and the heart of man go together."*
> John Ruskin

Activity 19. Positioning Objectives & Messages

Note: Read the following question all the way through, then re-read it to make your choice.

1. **Choose Your Positioning Objective.** Re-read the introduction to this activity, then recall your service statement and business image (from Activity 9) and your income-generating program (from Activity 11). Then, evaluating these with your current and future goals, determine your position by choosing one objective from the six that follow. The simpler, clearer, and more direct your objective, the easier it will be to create a successful promotional campaign. Are you ready to:

   a. Educate and inform your target clientele to create a demand for your service?

   b. Promote your specialty and gain visibility among your competitors?

   c. Seek to become regarded as an expert and/or a leader in your profession or community?

   d. Maintain your current comfortable position, visibility, and income level?

   e. Combine your service with another into a new concept or service, take a new approach, learn a new skill, or add a new service?

Empowering Vision

    f.   Stop what you are doing and begin something completely new?

        Fully explain your choice(s).

        Note: If you chose e or f, you will need to re-vision, set new goals, and rework your strategy. Do Activities 2, 9, 10, 11, 16, 17, 18, and 19 as needed.

2. **Name Your Business.** Now that you have determined your positioning objective, it's time to name or rename your business if you haven't already done so. Choose a name that best expresses your service, image, and objectives. Your business name is your first contact with your target clientele. Because it stimulates interest and trust, the name of your business can strongly affect the strength of your position. Be creative and tell your clientele, in a vocabulary familiar to them, what you really want them to know. Some guidelines for choosing a name are:

- Combine a descriptive word or phrase with your own name, keeping your image in mind. Consider these images: Bud's Garage; Hayward Automotive.

- Use common, descriptive words that clearly identify and generate interest in what you do: Boulder School of Massage Therapy.

- Choose clear, direct words rather than esoteric or obscure ones that may create confusion and could work against you: Attuning Your Energies.

- When using a location, street, town, or vicinity in your name, consider the consequences of a move: Rocky Mountain Art Works, Miami, Florida.

- Consider the vocabulary of your target clientele. What words create interest and trust for them?

- If your name identifies your service very specifically, what would happen if you expanded? Gold Rings by George.

- Short names are better than initials because they create feelings and images.

- Choose a name that is not too similar to a major competitor's.

- Choose a name that is easy to pronounce, preferably one with no more than four long or five short, clear words.

- People often choose one service over another because the name gives them a comfortable, trusting feeling. Consider the feeling projected by Kathryn Lawrence, Certified Massage Therapist vs. Kathy's Golden Touch.

- If you provide several diverse services, it may be best to use different names for each, especially if they appeal to different clients or project different images. Or, you could use different program names under the general title of your business.

Section 2. Marketing

    a. Take time to brainstorm and list possible names for your business. Choose one. Evaluate the way the name looks and sounds. Look up the definition of the words in the dictionary. Say it aloud, with your eyes closed. Hum it by syllables to experience the way it sounds and feels. Ask several people what they think when they hear the name. Be open to their responses.

    b. Contact both the Secretary of State and the Department of Revenue to discover if your chosen name is already in use. If so, you will need to choose another. Also, ask about the proper procedures for registering your name.

3. **Positioning Slogan.** In combination with your name, your positioning slogan will create a complete picture of what you offer. It will position you in the minds of your clientele and your competition. It can also be integrated into your name. For example, your name can define your niche: One-Hour Photo, Midas Muffler. A good slogan reinforces that niche in your clients' minds: "Ford has a better idea," or "You're in good hands with Allstate."

To create a slogan, first, evaluate the name of your business. What does it really tell your potential clientele about your service business? Does it say enough? If not, what more should it say? Now, write the name of your business:

> *Empowering Vision For Dreamers, Visionaries & Other Entrepreneurs*

Refer to your service statement (Activity 9, Question 1). Then, next to your name, write in fewer than seven words, exactly what you offer and want your clientele to know:

> *The business course that promotes success*

or

> *The first transformative business course*

Now, write a slogan that states your position in your service industry:

> *The first empowering business course*

or

> *Promoting mastery in business*

Empowering Vision

If you are not yet well-known, your slogan should state what you offer. If you are becoming known and want to take a strong position, create a slogan that will effectively state your position, specialty, or unique slant.

Your slogan is the simple statement that you will consistently use to describe your business. When people ask what you do, answer with your slogan: "We provide the business course that promotes success," or "We promote mastery in business." Place it on all your promotional materials—business cards, letterhead and envelopes, brochures, and ads. Remove it only when you have reached your goals or it no longer reflects your position, purpose, or image.

4. **Your Positioning Message Slant.** Review the client profile you created in Activity 16 and picture a typical client. Your positioning message will be written directly to your typical client. It will explain what she or he needs to know to make the decision to contact you. (Before you finalize your promotional message for your promotional materials, consult an editor for feedback and help.)

Read the following message slants and choose the one that fulfills the objective you identified in Question 1. Explain your choice. Consider what you want your typical client to think and feel while reading or hearing your positioning message.

   a. **Positioning Objective A—Educational and Informative:** Your service industry or particular kind of service is new, with few competitors. Your target clientele may never have heard of your kind of service. They may not know that a service exists to satisfy these particular needs or desires. You will want to explain clearly what you do, and how it will benefit them. Only then will they feel interested and trusting enough to sample your service.

   b. **Positioning Objective B—Persuasive:** Your service industry is becoming known, growing rapidly, and new competitors are emerging. Your target clientele may not yet understand the value of your service. Your goal is to explain its exceptional value and exactly how it addresses and satisfies their identified need. Then, whenever they need to use your service, they will think of you and will even refer others to you.

   c. **Positioning Objective C—Comparative:** Because your service industry has a strong position in society, there is much solid competition. Your target clients, therefore, are familiar with your service and may want to experience it. Perhaps, however, they do not know how to choose from all the available services. They may not even know the criteria by which to choose. Perhaps your skill level and confidence have developed to the level at which you can be considered an expert. Your message should explain your service, illuminate its benefits and highlight your specialty. Through your image and the description of your uniqueness, you will convince clients that your business is the only one to consider.

   d. **Positioning Objective D—Reminder-Oriented:** You are successful, your practice is full, and perhaps you are even regarded as an expert. Now you want to maintain your visibility or a high profile. Write your message to remind clients of your service. Give them a brief description of what you are doing and, perhaps, a reminder of how your work relates to a current issue of concern to them. Those who have thought about calling, but never have, might respond to a gentle nudge and finally contact you.

Your positioning message, combined with your name and slogan, will guide you in taking your unique position in your client service area. This will be your basic message, from which you can create longer statements for special promotions and proposals.

5. Based on your name, slogan, and the slant of your positioning message, write your basic message in just one paragraph. Do not be concerned with whether it is perfect or even well-written. For now, close your eyes, visualize your typical client, recall the benefits of your service, then open your eyes and write. (See Activity 24 for guidance in the design of your promotional materials.)

6. **Evaluate Existing Materials.** If you already have promotional materials, review them to evaluate the image they project, the position they state, and the slant of their message. Are you satisfied with your current message? If not, what will you do about it?

7. Describe the fears, resistances, or self-limiting patterns you experienced while completing this activity. What are you ready to do about them?

8. Reflect on the important points in this activity and describe how you feel empowered.

9. What must you learn and develop? What resources are you ready to draw upon? List the steps you will take and include dates, when appropriate.

◆

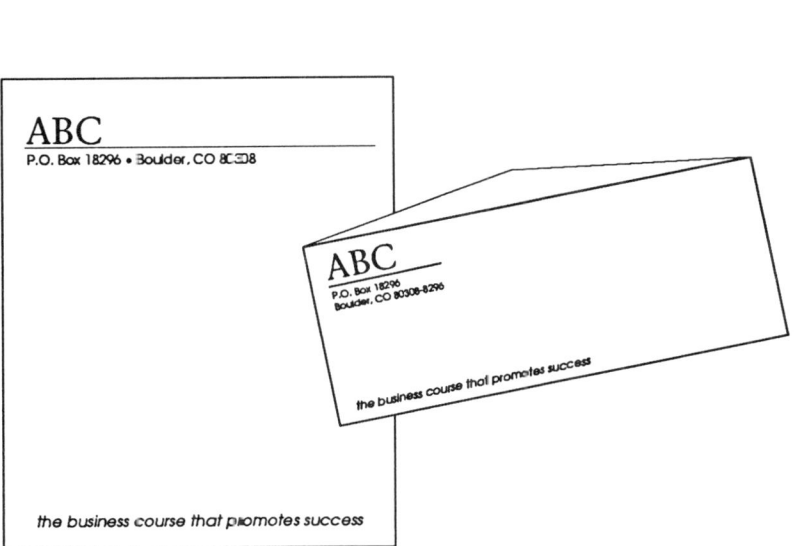

Empowering Vision

Promotional Campaign Options

A good promotion plan will create opportunities and thus increase your clientele and income. An effective plan will expose your service to more people so you can expand your business.

You have already identified some of the elements that will contribute to successful promotion. Many people resist promotional activities because they fear rejection. If this speaks to you, remember two points: first, if you have evaluated the market and know your target clientele, your promotion will focus on the segment of the population most likely to buy your service. Second, even if the "perfect" client turns you down, know that she or he simply does not need your service now. "No" is rarely a rejection of you personally; it just states the client's current choice, which can always change.

Objectivity is the key to successful and enjoyable marketing. Focus less on your expectations and more on the adventure, and see the gifts that result. Remember, you have chosen to be responsive to the changing needs and desires of the market rather than to your vulnerability. If you remain objective, promotion can be one of the most exciting activities in your business. You never know who you will meet and how your life will change as a result. A "cold call" can become your dearest friend.

"An artist knows his best brush."
Oriental Proverb

 Activity 20. Promotional Campaigns

The four categories of promotional campaigns are:

> A. Advertising
> B. Direct Sales
> C. Sales Promotions
> D. Public Relations

Each contains many options. For success, carefully choose a combination that is compatible with your values, abilities, and resources. Before you develop a comprehensive promotion plan or even one campaign, you need to evaluate thoroughly the available options and decide what will create the desired outcome.

Begin by titling one page with each of the following campaigns: Advertising, Direct Sales, Sales Promotions, and Public Relations. As you read each of the descriptions for each campaign, note your thoughts, ideas, and feelings on the appropriate sheet. At the end of each campaign description, you will find several questions to help you sort through your options. The practical and financial viability of the various campaigns will be evaluated later.

A. Advertising Campaign

1. **Advertising** provides non-personal, paid media presentations directed to either the general population (The *New York Times*) or to a specific market (*Yoga Journal*) in your client service area. Advertising will allow you to: 1) introduce your service to those not yet familiar with it; 2) gain name recognition for your business; 3) provide a reminder to those who have considered using your service; and 4) publicize specific promotions.

   If you decide to advertise, place ads in the media that will effectively expose you to your target clientele. Suggestions for evaluating these are given in parentheses following the description of each type of media. As you read each advertising option, list ideas on your Advertising page.

   Your local public library or university business library carries Standard Rate and Data Service (SRDS) directories. These carry demographic information and ad rates for newspapers, magazines, radio, and television. Ask your librarian for help in locating and using these directories.

   Most print and broadcast media have advertising sales representatives who, because they are paid a commission, want you to be satisfied. To develop an effective relationship, work with the same rep each time you buy advertising. If you are not satisfied, let the rep know or request another.

   Note: Printed media (a-e below) offer placement through display ads, classified ads, and calendar sections.

   a. Newspaper ads, though sometimes expensive and short lived, provide broad exposure to the general public. Because they give your business name recognition, newspapers tend to be most effective when you advertise regularly. (Consider starting with a daily classified ad and progressing to display ads as your funds increase.) Place your ad on the days and in the section of the paper your potential clients are most likely to read. Make a list of the newspapers and the sections your target clients read most consistently.

   b. Magazine ads are more expensive, yet have a longer life and provide exposure to a more select audience than newspapers. (Request placement where you think your target clients will most likely see them. At the very least, place your ad on the more visible right-hand page.) List the magazines and sections your clients read.

   c. Trade journals serve specific industries, usually over a national or large geographical area. They tend to be read thoroughly and are kept as resources. List the trade journals your typical clients are most likely to read.

   d. Free publications include community resource guides that are available free to the public at newsstands, stores, restaurants, institutes, etc. Evaluate and list these.

Empowering Vision

e. Newsletters provide low-cost exposure to a select readership and are usually well-targeted and inexpensive. List the newsletters read by your target clientele.

Note: Some of the media options listed above in a-e may sell Advertorial space. This paid space is designed to look like editorial copy. Sometimes the space is labeled *Advertisement* or *Advertorial*. Discuss this with an advertising sales representative to determine whether this is a good option for you. It may be more advantageous for you to write an article than pay for advertorial space.

f. Radio provides low-cost, brief exposure to your target audience. Ask the station's advertising sales representative to help you determine the time of day your target clientele listens. Radio advertising is most effective when it is frequent. You will need to write and produce a script in addition to paying air-time costs. List the radio stations that appeal to your clients and the times when they are most likely to listen.

g. Television is more expensive than radio but reaches more people. Make sure your clientele watches during the time periods you can afford. Call the stations of your choice for information. Remember to add the cost of producing a commercial to the quoted advertising rates.

h. Narrowcasting places ads on selected cable TV channels, in movie theaters, and on buses. Evaluate how you feel about any impact on your image.

i. Outdoor advertising includes billboards and benches. Give this option careful evaluation. These may not be appropriate for your service, and they may actually

Section 2. Marketing

hurt your image. To learn more about them, look for the name and telephone number of a contact listed on the billboard or bench.

j. Yellow Pages ads are expensive, but depending on your service, can provide unmatched exposure. Potential clients often use the telephone book as a resource. Most often they will call the company with the most impressive ad, the catchiest name, or the readily recognizable name. If you plan to be in the same area for several years and want to establish your business, it will pay to advertise in the Yellow Pages.

k. Computer bulletin boards are an up-and-coming way to gain exposure for your service. They are especially effective if you serve a regional, national, or international client base. Contact a computer dealer for information and the name of a local PC user's group.

l. Direct mail offers expensive, select coverage. You can do your own mailings or purchase an ad in a coupon book or directory. Another option is a direct response card deck, a group of ten to fifty postage-paid postcards with a common theme. (Many are listed in the SRDS volume, *Business Publications Rates and Data.*) Direct mail promotional pieces range from a postcard to a large envelope containing complete and elaborate information. Direct mail tends to have a low return (1-3 percent) unless it is preceded or followed by a telephone campaign or used with an especially well-targeted list.

The most effective use of direct mail is to offer a special discount, a free presentation, or a complimentary service. If you ask potential clients to write or call for in-depth information, you will be able to compile a targeted list of interested people for follow-up and future promotions. Compile your own mailing list from referrals, checks you receive, and attendance lists from your events. Include also the names of respondents to your ads, and other advertisers who could become clients. Buy or trade mailing lists of other businesses that serve your clientele.

You might also consider purchasing a list of names of likely clients from a mailing list company. Make sure the company guarantees an updated, clean list that is at least 98 percent accurate. To evaluate available lists, ask the reference librarian at your library for the SRDS volume called *Direct Mail List Rates and Data.* Or, call a local list broker, or ask other self-employed people in your client service area for ideas.

m. Posters and flyers are an inexpensive way to gain name recognition and publicity for an upcoming event. Place posters in locations that match your image and that expose you to your target clients. Postering services distribute posters on a one-time, regular, or intermittent basis at low cost. If poster exposure is right for you, this service is well worth the cost.

2. If possible, determine the advertising that is best for your business.

a. Evaluate your notes and ideas for advertising campaign options, 1a-m. Eliminate those that do not fit your image, needs or budget. Of those that remain, identify the one(s) appropriate for your goals.

b. Contact each medium or publication for their media kit or advertiser's packet. These include rate cards, ad sizes, circulation figures, and demographics. Ask for a sample publication if you don't have one.

c. Evaluate each medium, one at a time:

　1) Review each medium to determine if it is compatible with your professional image. If not, eliminate it from your list.

　2) Study each media kit. Evaluate the demographics and psychographics (see Activity 16) outlined in the kit to determine whether it matches your client profile. If not, eliminate it from your list. If the information you want is not included in the media kit, call the ad sales representative for more information.

　3) Organize the information using the Advertising Worksheet on Page 91.

　4) Convert the advertising cost to a figure you can compare with others: Divide the ad cost by the circulation. (For large magazines, figure the cost per 1,000 readers to obtain more manageable numbers.) For example, if a magazine has a circulation of 600,000 and a quarter-page ad costs $3,000, the cost per thousand is $3,000/600 or $5 per thousand subscribers. The cost per person for this ad is $.005. After you have completed these calculations for all your possibilities, review them to determine which ads are most cost effective.

d. Which media do you think will give you the best exposure to your target clientele? In order of priority identify the media you would like to use now or later.

e. Contact business owners who advertise in the media you are considering and ask about their success with their ads. Ask them to rate them on a scale of 1-10 for the number of inquiries and the number of actual sales. Ask what, if anything, they would change. Eliminate the media with low ratings.

f. Compare the remaining options on your Advertising Worksheet. Which do you think effectively and consistently keep your name highly visible to your target clientele? Which will give you the greatest exposure for the least expense? Review these from several perspectives: best exposure and placement, lowest cost, highest return, image, compatibility, best policies and terms, quality of relationship with the sales rep, and so forth.

Note: Your selection of media may change periodically, seasonally, or as your client base, promotional needs, and income fluctuate.

© Empowering Vision

Advertising Worksheet

Make copies of this form and use it as an original.

Name				
Readership				
Circulation				
Geographical Radius				
Publication Frequency				
Copy Due Date				
Release Date				
Ad Size				
Cost Per Ad				
Cost Per Person				
Average Response Rate				
Contact Person Phone #				

Empowering Vision

B. Direct Sales Campaign

A **direct sales** campaign is a one-to-one sales presentation to potential clients by you or your representative. Create a basic sales presentation, practice it, and present it enthusiastically. Always follow up every contact to determine if your service matches his or her needs.

Direct sales is, by far, the most effective way to generate interest. Ironically, it is also the option people resist the most. To sell, you must reach beyond fear, and perhaps far beyond any limitation you can imagine. As you address your resistance and reach out, you can provide yourself with both enhanced inner security and a comfortable lifestyle. (Refer to Activity 22 for guidance.)

Be sure to follow up on all calls and presentations, even when clients do not appear ready to buy. Send a note of appreciation. Caring enables relationships to grow.

1. On a sheet of paper labeled "Direct Sales," create a list called "Personal and Professional Supporters." List the mentors, colleagues, and professional and personal friends who love you, care about you, and want to see you succeed. Next, use a scale of 1-10 to rate each name. Consider the strength of their support and the breadth of their network. Eliminate the names rated 7 or less. This list will be one of your most valuable marketing tools. Update it periodically—whenever you re-vision or make new contacts.

   Contact each person on your list, explain what you are doing, and ask for ideas and names of people they know who might benefit from your presentation. Ask if they will provide you with a telephone introduction or letter of endorsement, if appropriate.

2. Create a list called "Potential Clients." These are people and organizations with whom you want to arrange a presentation. (The Yellow Pages can be a great resource.) Rate each on a scale of 1-10 and make contact with each, either by telephone (Activity 22) or by letter (Activity 23).

3. Create a list called "Client Leads." List any clients who might provide you with names of people they have talked to about your service and others who may be interested in your service. Ask if you can use their name, or if they will provide you with an introduction or a letter of endorsement.

4. Create a list called "Competitor Leads." List those competitors (Activity 17) who might refer clients. Include people with related services who may make referrals or with whom you can affiliate in some way.

5. Consider encouraging referrals by exchanging services or offering complimentary services or discounts to people you believe will broaden your exposure. (Activities 13 and 27 discuss discounts.) Use discretion so you will not tarnish your image or the value of your service.

6. If you choose direct sales, determine whether you are ready to do them yourself or whether you prefer to contract with someone. Perhaps you will want to do a little of both. You will be, by far, the most effective at selling your service. However, if you want help, consider:
   - Some people love sales and others are excellent networkers. If you know someone who fits this description and who believes in you and your service, consider a

contract with him/her for part-time sales. Or, offer a networking commission. This commission arrangement with several people will augment and enhance your own ongoing promotion. Another option is to join with others who need a promoter and hire someone together.

- Someone successful in telemarketing (telephone sales) can help to schedule appointments for you or someone who is comfortable with using the telephone can make calls to announce your upcoming events.

C. Sales Promotion Campaign

Sales promotions will increase your exposure and income through periodic and one-time promotions. Sales promotions include discount certificates, two-for-one offers, public displays, demonstrations, exhibits, and trade shows. These will provide ongoing support and periodic boosts to your other campaigns.

Remember that your best promotion tool is your personal presence. Use every opportunity to make personal presentations of your work. Talking to people you don't know may feel threatening, but so was taking your first step when you were a baby. The more presentations you make, the more comfortable, confident, and enthusiastic you will be. Commit to making several presentations in a specific period of time to help you overcome your anxiety. Begin with an audience of friends; then, when you are ready, contact others. Eventually, you will discover you are more comfortable than you ever thought possible.

1. With some kinds of services, it is appropriate to do a solo demonstration or display in a public or community location, or to rent space at exhibits, trade fairs, or trade shows. To learn about these opportunities, talk to someone with a similar service who knows your area. Also, inquire at the Chamber of Commerce, check the calendar sections of local newspapers, or contact your trade association.

    Evaluate whether these promotional methods are appropriate, cost effective, and within your financial and personal limits. Are you willing to do them yourself or will you need to hire someone else? Here are some more ideas:

    a. Find out which upcoming trade fairs or shows in your client service area may be appropriate for you. Request exhibitors' and speakers' information. Such events are advertised in local papers and trade journals and are announced by professional membership organizations. Your participation or attendance allows you to make valuable contacts, evaluate the competition, and stay current with industry trends. Speaking at these enhances your credibility, and being an exhibitor can greatly increase your exposure, and your confidence.

    b. If appropriate for your service, list the shopping centers, malls, or other locations in your client service area where you can give demonstrations. Many centers have

Empowering Vision

        begun organizing and promoting their own shows and exhibits and are eager to hear from you. Select the ones at which you would feel comfortable doing a promotion. Then, call the center's executive offices for details on cost, dates and times, procedures, display dimensions, demographics, and psychographics, so that you can make a solid decision. Demonstrate with colleagues; it is easier, more fun, and costs less.

    c. Organize the information on trade fairs, exhibitions, shows, and shopping center demonstrations so that you can compare them. Evaluate these to select the events that will be most beneficial.

2. If it seems appropriate, offer discounted sessions or professional exchanges to people who can provide you with greater exposure. This can be an effective, low-cost way to increase your exposure. Determine how many hours per week or month you will allocate for these arrangements. Because you will still have your regular program costs, refer to Activity 13, Discounts, and Activity 32, Break-even Calculation, to evaluate their financial and administrative impact. Be sure to exchange checks for all trades.

3. Promote gift certificates during seasonal low periods, holidays, or whenever you want to increase your exposure. Gift certificates should generally be offered at your regular price. When you want to increase your exposure and income, offer an extended or month-long special, such as a two-for-one package (make one appointment now and receive another several weeks later). You might offer a special when you want to encourage a new or wavering client to make another appointment.

    a. Offer discounted or complimentary gift certificates to your favorite and most loyal clients. Keep track of how often you provide your service to regular clients, then, offer them a complimentary session or a gift certificate for a friend every x number of appointments. Think of other ideas. With creativity and organization, you really can enjoy promotion.

    b. Refer to B. Direct Sales, 1-5. From these lists, select people to whom you want to offer a gift certificate, then contact these people.

    c. Provide select people with gift or discount certificates that they can give friends and associates. Or, you might want to call the people they recommend, explain your service and offer a gift certificate, or a discounted or complimentary service. (Keep track of all promotional discounts. Your accountant may be able to deduct them for tax purposes. See Activities 13 and 27.)

Note: Remember that word-of-mouth is your best exposure. When you provide a quality service, your clients will tell others about what you do. In addition, give yourself every opportunity to talk about your work. (see Networking, Question 2, Page 96.) When people repeatedly hear the name of your business, they become more comfortable with it and may decide to call you.

4. Meet with someone experienced in sales promotions who understands your work and is creative. Or, create a group of close associates and friends to devise various ways of offering sales promotions, discounts, and complimentary services. Eliminate ideas that are not appropriate, or that do not feel right. List the rest in order of priority and begin making contacts.

5. Compile and maintain a mailing list. Transfer names, addresses, and telephone numbers from all client checks, add all networking leads you receive, and include anyone you feel would be appropriate. Use this list for future mailings. Keep it up-to-date by printing "Address Correction Requested" on your mailing envelope. (Check with your post office for costs and rules.)

D. Public Relations Campaign

Public Relations is the art of developing public awareness and good will for your business through media interviews, press releases, and networking. Unlike advertising, you do not pay for this exposure. Like advertising, public relations allows you to: 1) explain your service in detail to those who may not be familiar with it; 2) gain further name recognition for your business; 3) further interest those who have considered using your service; and 4) publicize upcoming events and campaigns.

1. Publicity is informative, newsworthy information issued with the goal of attracting public interest or support. Both the print and broadcast media are constantly looking for interesting news material. Using this free advertising vehicle allows you to increase your exposure with little or no increase in expenses.

    a. Work with a writer to create press releases. Send a press release every time you have news. If you pass a milestone in your career, win an award or an election, hire or affiliate with someone new, sign a contract with a large client, or move your office, this is news. Send one release for each event, rather than one with several events. Make sure the information you include is newsworthy. Format it as a short news piece. (If you need guidelines, check with the news department of your local papers and magazines.) Because publications receive so many releases, there is no guarantee they will include your information, but persistence pays off. Watch to see if your press releases are printed. Keep them in a file for future use as testimonials. Remember to write the date and source on each.

    b. Ask others to write about you. Review Question 1, Page 87 and list the publications your target clients read. Evaluate articles to determine which columnists or reporters you like best. Contact them a month before your upcoming event to see if they would like to write an article about your service. Or ask a friend with media contacts to provide you with an introduction.

    c. Refer to your list of trade journals on Page 87. Contact editors to suggest they write an article about the new technique, theory, or approach you have learned or developed. Trade journals and consumer magazines often pay for articles. (If you aren't confident with your writing skills, hire a professional writer to help.)

d. Consider writing a regular column. If you have enough interesting and relevant information and the writing ability to publish regularly, consider approaching the editor of the appropriate section of a newspaper, magazine, journal, or newsletter.

e. Create your own newsletter. This can be expensive, but if you have regular, repeat clients, you can generate good will and promote your products and services by providing valuable and relevant information. Depending on your intention and image, you might ask for a nominal annual subscription fee or accept paid advertising.

f. Radio and television talk shows provide excellent exposure, especially if the exposure is coordinated with an event you have planned. Watch or listen to your local stations to determine which ones would be most interested in your field. Contact show hosts or program directors. Be aware that some talk show hosts tend to be confrontive with their guests. If you are not at ease with this, or lack experience in a live interview format, you might want to seek less controversial programs at first.

Regular programming is scheduled months in advance, so you will need to make initial contacts several months before your planned promotion. Listen to the program to become familiar with the host's style. Local cable stations are easier to begin with than network stations. Ask friends for the names of media contacts. Before your show is recorded, ask the program manager to provide you with a tape of the broadcast.

g. If appropriate for your professional goals, status and image, and if you can appeal to a wide audience, consider developing a regular radio or television show. The rapid growth of cable television is providing new arenas for broadcast publicity. Dozens of community access stations are actively seeking educational programming ideas. If your service or field of expertise fits the community or consumer education format, consider writing a program proposal. Some stations charge for this exposure, but it can still be cost effective, depending on your service and your positioning objectives. Contact the stations in your area for details.

h. If you are comfortable and skilled with public speaking, contact local clubs, groups, and organizations whose members match your client profile. Many are looking for interesting programs for monthly meetings. You probably will not be paid, but you will have an opportunity to meet potential clients and practice your speaking skills.

i. Give free or low-cost seminars to introduce people to your service. Consider putting together a program with other professionals to gain exposure to each other's clientele. Add the names of those attending to your mailing list.

2. **Networking** is a valuable function of business because it offers an easy way to make professional contacts. Because your best promotion is your personal presence, networking allows you

to make new contacts and to practice your sales presentation without the pressure of sales. Most networking contacts may not lead directly to new clients quickly, however, so these should not be relied upon as an alternative to sales.

a. Business and professional groups meet to support each other. Joining the right associations, clubs, and groups can give you support and exposure. Typical ones include: the Chamber of Commerce, Leads and Networking Groups, Win/Win Business Forums, Salesmen with a Purpose (SWAP), Business and Professional Women's (BPW) clubs, and church groups. Give yourself every opportunity to talk about what you do. Consider serving on the board of directors of a for-profit organization or a high profile, not-for-profit organization. Or, join a service club (such as Rotary, Lions, or Zonta). This is an excellent way to learn about business, gain exposure, have fun, and help your community.

b. Have an open house to introduce yourself to your business neighbors and potential clients. Have a drawing to give a complimentary session, if appropriate for your service.

c. Take the time to talk to people. When you meet someone who fits your client profile and with whom you might like to work, offer a discounted session. There are many opportunities to meet people, from parties and social events to standing in line at the market, or while riding the bus. One of the first questions people tend to ask is, "What do you do?" Some of the best sales opportunities occur at moments like these. Be open to opportunities, and enjoy the surprises that result. Always keep your business card handy, ask for theirs, and follow-up with a phone call or note in the mail to establish a relationship. Add these people to your mailing list.

In Activity 21, Promotion Plan, you will organize all your ideas from this activity into the promotion plan that is right for you.

So, how did it go?

1. How do you feel about promotion now? How will these feelings enhance your business success? What fears, resistances, or self-limiting patterns were dissolved? What changes are you ready to make? What support do you need? How are you ready to receive this?

2. Reflect on the important points in this activity and describe how you feel empowered.

3. In retrospect, what do you realize you already knew about promotion?

4. What must you learn and develop? What resources are you ready to draw on? List the steps you will take and include dates, when appropriate.

◆

Developing Your Promotion Plan

Your promotion plan is a consolidation of ideas from the four promotional campaigns—advertising, direct sales, sales promotions, and public relations—identified in Activity 20. As you begin organizing your promotion plan, choose only those options that excite you, and those for which you have time and money.

The key to successful promotion lies in knowing what you are willing to do and what you can afford. Use your resources to empower yourself to promote using the right mix of campaign options. The following activity will help you devise a promotional plan that reflects your positioning objectives, budget, and willingness.

Before you design your campaign options into a plan, consider:

- New business owners often underadvertise because they don't have enough, or think they don't have enough, money. Name recognition is essential, and periodic or reg-ular advertising creates recognition. As suggested, even a small classified ad can produce good results. If you do advertise, choose the one or two most appropriate media. Advertise in several media at the same time or in the same media often enough so that people will begin to recognize your business name. To determine your ad results, run the same ad regularly for four months. Keep track of inquiries so you can evaluate which ads provide the best return.

- Five percent of your projected gross income should be an adequate initial advertising budget. Once you are established, your advertising costs should range from 2 to 5 percent.

- Remember that networking is an excellent way to gain exposure and name recognition. People who attend meetings and conferences are like you: they may turn out to be good friends or great sources of referrals. Attend professional and social events to discover what others are doing and how networking or collaboration can create benefit and support for all. You'll find these events listed in the calendars of events in community presses, local newspapers, and in trade journals. Most clubs and organizations invite you to attend one free meeting to determine your interest.

- The more energy and focus you put into your promotional activities, the greater your momentum and return. Although promotion takes time, you do not have to do it all yourself. Promotion can be more enjoyable when you are involved with others.

*"Communication is to relationship
as breathing is to life."*
Virginia Satir

Section 2. Marketing

📣 Activity 21. Promotion Plan

1. **Program title.** Title and describe your program from Activity 11. If you have more than one program, remember to develop a different promotion plan for each.

2. **Marketing goals.** Review Activity 19, Positioning Objectives & Messages, then state the goal of your current promotion plan. For example, "sign up thirty people for the March 13 seminar." Determine this promotion's beginning and ending dates (begin February 5, stop on March 10).

3. **Income goals.** Determine the amount of income you want this plan to generate. Divide your fee into total income to get the number of sales or clients you need to obtain that income. How many clients do you have now? How many more will you need in order to reach your income goal?

4. **Time.** Determine the number of hours you have available each week for this promotion and for giving discounted and complimentary services. Use Activity 7, Master Schedule, to schedule specific times for promotional activities. Consider how much more work you want and are willing to handle. Consider how the additional work will affect your current workload, personal life, and energy level.

5. **Themes.** With your positioning objective in mind, determine the theme of your promotion. Even routine events can be spruced up with a theme. Some examples are:

    - Regular or periodic seminars, courses, or workshops
    - Seasonal (spring, winter, summer, fall)
    - Holiday (Christmas, Valentine's Day)
    - A gift certificate
    - Exposure to something new, different, or exciting
    - An exciting opportunity
    - A new resolution, revitalized commitment, or new beginning.

    Add your ideas and ask others for ideas. Consider whatever is appropriate for your current promotional objectives, budget, and the season of your promotion. Keep notes of ideas that you want to use in the future.

6. **Evaluate campaign options.** Read your notes from each of the four campaigns in Activity 20, Promotional Campaigns, and:

    a. Rate each option for excitement, willingness, and affordability.

    b. Eliminate options with a rating below 8.

    c. Which options remain? Evaluate these for efficient use of time, energy, and money. Choose the most effective. List in order of priority.

d. Beginning with your favorite or highest rated option, list the steps necessary to carry the idea to completion. Include dates and costs. If you think of ideas for other campaigns, include them in your notes.

7. **Promotional materials.** List the promotional materials (current, new, or revised) you want for each campaign. Consider business cards, brochures, flyers, posters, gift certificates, discount certificates, advertisements, letterhead, and cover letters. If you must create new promotional pieces, refer to Activity 24, Planning Promotional Materials. Add these costs to your budget.

8. **Budget.**

   a. Refer to your program budget from Activities 5 and 11. Total your projected costs for advertising, promotional materials, networking, and sales commissions as appropriate.

   b. Total the costs for all campaigns. Compare this figure with your program budget total from Activity 11. If there is a difference, evaluate and make necessary adjustments. Adjust program budget figures as appropriate.

   c. Evaluate whether it is realistic to allocate this amount of money to promotional activities. If not, evaluate each campaign, and eliminate those that may not produce the results you want. Can you schedule the more expensive campaigns later when your increased cash flow will cover the costs? Make adjustments until you are sure you are not overextending yourself.

9. **Promotion plan.** Refer to the CPM Chart in Activity 6. Using this format, schedule the activities of each promotional campaign on its own track, within the time period of your current marketing objectives (from Questions 2-8). Evaluate the sequence of steps in each campaign. Make sure they are complete and in the appropriate order, and that you've allocated a realistic amount of time for each step and between all activities. Everything tends to take longer than you think. Remember also that mistakes happen, sometimes at the most inconvenient times. Make adjustments as appropriate.

10. **CPM Chart.** Integrate the activities from your Promotion Plan, Question 9, into their sequences onto the marketing track of the CPM Chart you prepared in Activity 6. Compare your marketing activities with the activities in the remaining tracks and with activities scheduled in your appointment book, and personal activities. Is this manageable? Will your ongoing business and personal activities support this promotion? If not, determine the activities to adjust or eliminate, if only temporarily. Perhaps you need assistance. If so, what will it be and how will you get it? Evaluate your plan and make adjustments until you are certain it will work.

11. Repeat Questions 1-10 for your other programs.

12. Describe the fears, resistances, or self-limiting patterns you experienced while completing this activity. What will you do about them?

13. Reflect on the important points in this activity and describe the clarity you have gained. How will this affect your marketing abilities?

14. What must you learn and develop? What resources will you draw on to build strength? What steps will you take to fulfill these?

    Note: Even when your workload and income have reached your preferred levels, maintain this stability by making regular networking contacts, placing ads for greater name recognition, following up on referrals and leads, and making regular sales calls.

◆

$E = mc^2$

"Whatever you can do,
or dream you can,
begin it.
Boldness has genius,
power and magic in it.
Begin it now."
Goethe

Additional Marketing Information

Successful promoters realize that they are always marketing, whether through casual conversations at a party or formal presentations at a business conference. Unless you are a naturally eloquent speaker and know your material well, benefiting from marketing opportunities will require preparation. Each time you talk about your business, you will want to appear enthusiastic, knowledgeable, and sincere. If you develop presentations for all situations (using Activities 22 and 23), and learn to anticipate possible responses, questions, or concerns, you will rarely be at a loss for words, and the experience will be enjoyable.

Introduction to Sales

Sales is a wonderful way, and in fact, the only way to ensure that those clients who are ready to buy your service will know about it, use it, and receive its benefits. A sales conversation gives prospective clients the opportunity to hear about something that is of value to them. In addition, through sales, you provide yourself with the opportunity to meet and enjoy people you would not otherwise meet. In the process, you give your clients the most valued of all services—someone who is enthusiastic and who cares.

Close your eyes for a moment, and visualize several typical clients, two people who are ready to buy your service. Picture yourself describing to them the programs that you offer. Listen to how you sound, and listen to their questions and responses. Feel their interest level rising. Imagine them telling you how they appreciate finding someone who understands their needs. See yourself and these people agreeing on a time for their first appointment—the first, perhaps, of many. When you part, notice that all of you feel pleased and satisfied.

Now visualize yourself describing your program to two other people. See yourself listening and responding to their questions. Visualize them telling you they do not experience the need for your service.

This is what selling is about. It is the perfect "win-win" situation, regardless of the outcome: you either create a solid relationship, based on a clear understanding, or you enjoy a one-time conversation with someone you may not otherwise have met. Even when you are sure someone needs your service, she or he won't always agree. You will talk to more people who are not ready to buy than to people who are. If you have taken the time to create a program that is truly valuable and of high quality, if you know that you have carefully defined your target clientele and positioned yourself in your industry, and if you do not expect everyone to buy your service, then sales will be fun and profitable.

Most people consider sales a process of convincing others to buy. Yet, sales relationships and communications are changing as we realize that the quality of the communication is as important as the outcome. Indeed, the quality of the communication creates the outcome.

The bottom line in sales, then, is creating a mutually beneficial relationship. Through conversation, you determine your potential clients' needs and interests; if their responses indicate a need, you explain how your service program will benefit them.

The Sales Process below will help you design a clear sales presentation. Read it, study it, and use Activity 22, Direct Sales, to create your basic presentation.

The Sales Process

Use the following outline as a guide for preparing sales presentations.

1. **Identify, list, and contact your prospects.** Create a Prospective Client Profile (see Page 105) and make copies. Complete a form for each prospect. Telephone or, if appropriate, visit each client. Make notes on your log each time you make contact. File each prospect's profile sheets together in a note card box, file folder (see Activity 15), or binder.

2. **Qualify.** Make sure the prospect fits your client profile and has needs that are applicable to your business. The best way to discover this and other relevant information about your prospects' needs is to ask. Evaluate the following two ways of asking questions:

   a. *Closed questions* require a "yes" or "no" answer. This kind of question will help you determine if you are speaking to someone receptive to your service. Use this kind of question to learn factual information about his or her business, his or her current use of similar services, and any other information that is easily covered with a simple "yes" or "no." An example of a closed question is: "Do you like the service you are using?"

   b. *Open questions* require the client to provide more information. Any question beginning with who, what, when, where, why, or how is an open question. For example: "What do you like about the service you are using?" or "What more do you want from the service you are using?"

3. **Determine prospect's needs.** To become familiar with your prospects and to understand each one's unique situation, determine their specific needs and desires. Ask pertinent questions, both closed and open, to learn more about the prospect's unique needs. This will help you know if your service matches those needs, and if so, how best to serve them. The excitement of the sales process is that you never know what to expect—the surprise is only a conversation away.

4. **Deliver your presentation.** Describe the major features of your service that apply to the prospect's stated needs or desires. Highlight the few points that address his or her most important needs. Discuss only those features that pertain to the prospect's circumstances.

5. **Know your competition.** Be familiar with competitors in case a prospect asks about other's services (see Activity 17, Competition). Know the similarities and differences between their services and yours.

6. **Respond to objections.** Be open to objections—they provide opportunities to further tailor your presentation to the prospect's concerns and interests. An objection means that you may have an opportunity to see this prospect become a client! As you become experienced with sales, you will know which objections may arise and will be better prepared to respond. Write down new objections that clients bring up so you can incorporate responses into your presentation. Always answer objections, but don't bring them up yourself.

7. **The Closing.** During your presentation, if the prospect is interested, she or he will convey this to you through positive statements and tone of voice. These can include: agreement with your assessment of the prospect's needs and benefits ("I like that feature; it sounds great."); concern with details ("How soon can we start? How long will it take?"); and recitation of the benefits back to you ("We can accomplish this objective in only eight sessions?"). At this point, you can ask for the sale with an open question that assumes the sale is made ("Yes; when shall we begin?"). Or, you can give the client a choice ("Shall we begin on Tuesday or Thursday?"). The close requires your initiation; begin as soon as you detect any closing signals. Again, listen to your client.

   Some clients take time—even months—to develop. Persevere. If your prospect is open, but is not ready or able to buy now, ask what further information he or she needs to make a decision. Set up the next meeting or a time to call back, even if it is in six months. Make sure you keep the individual's name, name of the business, address, phone number, and basic identifying information in a good filing system—a database, a binder filled with log sheets, or 8-1/2" x 11" file folders. Include each prospect on your mailing list, when appropriate. Adapt the Prospective Client Profile form that follows or create your own.

8. **Follow-up.** Follow-up gestures, such as a note in the mail or a telephone call, create a more solid relationship and greater potential for referrals. Maintaining a log will help refresh your memory about previous conversations. A log will also remind you of the next action with this client.

> *"If you don't say what you mean,*
> *you'll never mean what you say."*
> The Last Emperor

Prospective Client Profile Form

Make copies of this form and use it as an original.

© Empowering Vision

Date:
Contact name: Title:
Name of business:
Address:
Phone (Day):   (Evening):
Type of business:
Referred by:
Telephone/visit mailing log:
Follow-up action required:
Referrals:

Note: This profile should indicate the dates of all contacts and serve as a summary of what was discussed or mailed.

Direct Sales Presentations

Often, when the word "sales" is spoken, it is with an unpleasant tone. Many people are afraid to sell, because more often than not, the prospect says "no." Negative responses tend to trigger fear of non-support and the feeling of rejection, and many find it difficult to continue making calls. They often have to take a break, get some distance, and continue reaching out again only when they feel stronger. Clearly, sales is a powerful opportunity to move beyond the fear of rejection. The most effective sales people do.

Direct sales calls can be "cold calls," which are contacts with prospects with whom you have had no prior contact. However, in a service business, you want to contact only well-targeted and qualified prospects, as described in Activity 16, Client Profile, and The Sales Process, Page 103. Such contacts are more aptly called "warm calls," because the prospects are likely to be interested and eager to talk to you.

Even though warm calls are less intimidating than cold calls, they still challenge most people. Fortunately, preparation and practice eliminate anxiety. Remember that the people you call are likely to be ready for your service. A call provides them with information they want. To interest your prospect, state your purpose immediately, be engaging, and most of all, be sensitive. Be friendly, and use your prospect's name. You want to interest your prospect so that she or he either agrees to use your service or makes an appointment to discuss it further. In addition, your prospective client is far more likely to be interested in what you say if you communicate easily about your service. Carefully reread The Sales Process.

Remember, when talking on the telephone, you have only your words and the sound of your voice to convey your message. For immediate feedback, set a mirror in front of you and watch your face as you speak. Are you smiling, relaxed, open, friendly? Do you like what you see? What you see is what your prospect hears. Once you have established a warm, pleasant tone, practice your presentation. Be brief and to the point without sounding rushed. Whenever possible, familiarize yourself with your prospect before you call. That way, you can better know how your service will benefit his or her unique needs.

With direct sales calls, you are involved in what is called "a numbers game." It takes several, and sometimes, many calls before you get a positive response, depending on how specifically you targeted your prospective clients. Expect that it will take time, and if you persevere, you will obtain the results you want.

Use the following activity as a guide to help you follow up on referrals, chance meetings, cold calls, and promotional materials you have mailed.

*"That which is dynamic is powerful, forceful,
filled with energy, and leads to change."*
Catherine Ponder

Activity 22. Direct Sales—Phone Calls or Visits

1. Introduce yourself, state your line of service. Smile as you speak. Remember that you have about thirty seconds to get your prospect's attention.

2. Identify your contact point: referral, chance meeting, promotional materials you mailed. If you are making a cold call, explain how you found the prospect's name. Determine if the prospect has time to talk with you now. If not, determine if you can schedule another time to talk.

3. If you have already sent materials, ask your prospect if she or he has received them. Be prepared to respond to any of the following possibilities:

    a. Received materials, did not read, has no interest.
    b. Received materials, read, has no interest.
    c. Received materials, did not read, has interest.
    d. Received materials, read, has interest.
    e. Hasn't received materials.

4. Determine your prospect's familiarity with your service, and from his or her response, explain your service. Determine needs, tailor your presentation to these needs, and remember to include your positioning objective and message (from Activity 19). Periodically ask for comments and questions.

5. From the prospect's comments, describe what you think she or he will receive from using your service. If you are not sure, describe some benefits others with similiar needs have received.

6. Ask if your prospect is ready to use your service, wants to hear more, or receive a complimentary session (if appropriate). Be prepared for any of the following possibilities:

    a. Your prospect is ready to buy your service.
    b. Your prospect will consider using your service.
    c. Your prospect will make referrals to you.
    d. You will become part of each other's referral network.
    e. Your prospect does not want your service.

7. If your prospect says no, ask for an explanation and, if it feels right, ask if you may call at a later date. Follow up; keep records; keep a mailing list. If she or he says yes, set a date and time.

8. Write a strategy for leaving your message on answering machines.

9. Practice your presentation aloud several times. Then, present it to a friend, colleague, or professional coach. Revise it as needed.

10. Describe the fears, resistances, or self-limiting patterns that you experienced while completing this activity. What are you ready to do about them?

Empowering Vision

11. Reflect on the important points in this activity and describe how you feel empowered.

12. In retrospect, what do you realize you already knew about creating sales presentations?

13. What must you learn and develop? What resources are you ready to draw on? List the steps you will take and include dates, when appropriate.

◆

*"Whenever you feel down or discouraged,
reach out, inspire someone,
and in the process you will be inspired."*
Marianne Weidlein

Section 2. Marketing

How to Write a Cover Letter

A cover letter accompanies other information and introduces you and your service to a prospective client. The most effective cover letter begins by attracting the reader's interest, then states the desired response. A clear and interesting letter will attract and hold the reader's attention. Even if your writing skills are good, ask for feedback from an editor before mailing your cover letter. A sample letter may be found on Page 110.

Activity 23. How to Write a Cover Letter

1. Begin by explaining why you are writing. State the need or desire you think the prospect has in relation to your service. Briefly explain how the prospect will benefit.

2. Introduce yourself and briefly explain your qualifications and your service.

3. Ask the prospect to do something: call you, read the enclosure, consider something you have proposed.

4. Thank the prospect for reading your letter and enclosure. Explain when and how you will make contact to:

   a. Discuss your idea in detail
   b. Answer specific questions
   c. Discuss possible arrangements to give your presentation
   d. Talk about how you can work together.

   If you are mailing a large volume of letters, you may not intend to follow up on each one. If so, ask interested prospects to contact you or return an enclosure. If you intend to follow up on each personally, you may prefer to send a smaller number of letters.

5. Read your letter aloud and edit it several times. Then read it aloud to a friend, colleague, or mentor. Or, give it to a writer/editor for a final edit.

6. Make sure it is neatly typed, with no spelling errors, and that you are as proud of how it looks as you are of what it says.

7. Be sure to follow up as stated.

◆

Sample Cover Letter

*a*imari Press

May 1, 1991

Dear Friend

As you use this course manual, do you notice that you want guidance and feedback? Help is just a letter away.

This manual accompanies the *Empowering Vision* course currently available in Colorado. If you are located outside Colorado, we encourage you to benefit from the complete course and to help others use it by becoming an Empowering Vision facilitator.

Following training, which includes an intensive version of the complete course, you will receive individualized instruction. Upon certification as an Empowering Vision facilitator, you receive a Facilitator's Manual containing detailed facilitation plans and everything you need to successfully conduct Empowering Vision classes in your area.

For details, write to me, care of the publisher at the address below. We are committed to your success.

Sincerely

Marianne Weidlein

——— P.O. Box 18296 • Boulder, Colorado 80308-8296 • (303) 442-0681 ———

Developing Promotional Materials

As previously stated, promotional materials communicate your service, specialty, quality, image, and position, as well as the benefits your clientele will receive. An effective promotional piece not only informs your target clientele that you are in business, it brings them to your door. It reveals your legitimacy, states your fees, and describes your methods. An effective promotional piece:

- States your business name, specialty, and position

- Displays a brief outline of your program

- Indicates how your service will satisfy your client's needs or desires

- Explains how your service will facilitate change from the client's current situation to his or her preferred situation

- Tells your target client that you are qualified and credible, that you understand his or her needs and values, and that your service is the one for them.

Your promotional materials should clearly state your service and identify the characteristics that distinguish it from similar services. From Activity 9, Your Service, Quality & Image, Question 5, promote your strongest benefits and features, using language your clients will understand. Include a simple program outline, if appropriate, and, using Activity 19, Positioning Objectives & Messages, Question 4, write your promotional message in simple, direct terms.

Unless you are skilled in writing, typesetting, and graphics, you will need to figure a budget for these professional services for your business cards, letterhead, brochures, flyers, and other printed materials. Make sure all your materials are typeset, not typewritten. Typewritten promotional pieces, even flyers, lack professionalism and tend to create questions about credibility. The planning sheets in this activity will help you summarize your marketing objectives, as well as provide you with specific information about conveying your service, quality, image, and position to the professionals that help you. You can do much of the planning yourself, using the following activity.

Begin by collecting samples of printed materials, especially those of your competitors. Note the features that most appeal to you. Be clear about the reasons for your choices. Obtain samples of type styles from a printer, typesetter, or graphic art supply store. Obtain color and paper samples from a printer. Before you meet with consultants, be clear about what you want to accomplish. This will save you time, money, and energy.

Always review rough drafts before final drafts are prepared. Check final drafts before they are typeset, and make sure camera-ready artwork is finished. Check everything again before the piece is printed. At the camera-ready stage, withhold final approval until you are able to visualize the completed piece by making a photocopy and folding it. At each stage, you are responsible for payment, once you have given your approval, even if there is an error you overlooked.

Empowering Vision

✍ Activity 24. Planning Promotional Materials

Note: Keep these planning sheets as originals, and make copies as needed. Repeat this activity for each promotional piece.

1. What is the major goal of this promotion?

2. To whom is this promotion addressed?

   ____ former clients   ____ other professionals   ____ current clients
   ____ organizations   ____ potential clients   ____ purchased mailing list

3. What type of promotional piece(s) do you need? Check the ones you are designing now.

   ____ business cards/appointment cards   ____ postcard
   ____ brochure   ____ booklet/pamphlet
   ____ flyer   ____ book/manual
   ____ newsletter   ____ other: _____
   ____ letterhead/envelopes

4. Do you currently have promotional materials? _____ No _____ Yes (please attach). If yes, determine why these materials appeal to you. Do you like the paper, printing, graphics, layout, size, etc.? Identify any qualities that you dislike.

5. What is your positioning objective?

   ____ To educate, inform, and create a demand for your service
   ____ To promote your specialty and gain visibility in a rapidly growing or changing industry
   ____ To seek expert/leader status in profession/community
   ____ To maintain current position and income level.

6. Business Description: (Activities and questions are referred to in abbreviated form. (For example: "A19, Q1" means Activity 19, Question 1.)

   a. Name of business (A19,Q2) _____

   b. Positioning slogan (A19,Q3) _____

   c. Program name (A11,Q1) _____

   d. Target clientele (A16,Q2) _____

   e. Target clientele's current state (A11,Q4) _____

   f. Target clientele's preferred state (A11,Q4) _____

Section 2. Marketing

g. Specify four program benefits (A11,Q5)
   Note: All benefits should be stated in positive terms.

   _____

   _____

   _____

   _____

7. Program details for inclusion in promotional piece:

   a. Hours _____

   b. Dates _____

   c. Location _____

   d. Cost/Deposit _____

   e. Contact person _____

   f. Address _____

   g. Phone _____

   h. Biographical information (use a separate sheet) _____

   i. Message: Type of message (A19,Q4) (you may check more than one): Attach the message you wrote in A19, Q4.

   _____ Educational/Informative _____ Persuasive _____ Comparative _____ Reminder

   j. Testimonials: Attach strong comments from your clients about your service. (Whenever possible, use names, not initials, and include the client's profession or business name.)

8. How do you want your client to respond to this promotional piece (return card, telephone, or write for more information, etc.)?

9. When do you want these materials? (Production of a one-page flyer takes about a week; a brochure, depending on complexity, can take a month or more.)

10. What is the budget for these promotional materials? (A21,Q8)?

11. Do you plan to use this piece ____ one time or ____ multiple times? If multiple use is planned, will you need an ____ insert you can revise to update prices or dates?

12. For what period of time do you intend this piece to meet your needs?
    ____ 3 months   ____ 6 months   ____ 1 year   ____ other _____

13. How many will you need for this promotion?
    ____ 100-500   ____ 500-1,000   ____ 1,000-5,000   ____ 5,000-10,000   ____ 10,000+

14. Underline the words that describe your desired image and add your own.

    | expensive | masculine | refined | aware |
    | informal | high-tech | knowledgeable | straightforward |
    | professional | understanding | slick | responsive |
    | feminine | leader | spiritual | respectful |
    | affordable | caring | expert | dependable |
    | formal | flashy | intelligent | skilled |
    | strong | elegant | light | experienced |

15. Considering cost, time, and quality, which of the following options do you prefer for this piece?

    Top line package: quality paper, custom inks, photographs and/or custom graphics, special folding, non-standard size (lengthy turnaround)

    Mid-range package: good paper, special inks, graphics

    Budget package: ordinary paper, black/color-of-the-day ink, fast turnaround (instant printer)

16. How do you want the piece to look? (A graphic artist, printer, and writer should help with this.)

    ____ % text + ____ % illustration + ____ % photographs + ____ % return card + ____ % other = 100%

    Size: ____ 8½ x 11 (letter size)   Style: ____ vertical   ____ self-mailer
          ____ 8½ x 14 (legal size)   ____ horizontal   ____ mailed in envelope
          ____ 11 x 17 (tabloid)   ____ flat (no folds)   ____ with cover letter
          ____ 8½ x 5½   ____ other _____
          ____ single-sided
          ____ double-sided   ____ 1-fold to _____ (size)
          ____ multiple pages   ____ 2-fold to _____ (size)
          ____ # of pages   ____ 3-fold to _____ (size)

Paper: **Type**   Color

   ___ glossy   ___ white

   ___ linen   ___ off-white

   ___ parchment   ___ colored

   ___ textured   ___ pastel

   ___ cover stock   ___ bright

   ___ text weight

   ___ recycled

Ink: ___ black only   ___ one PMS color   ___ two PMS colors

      ___ three PMS colors ___ other_____   ___ four (Process) colors

Note: If you aren't satisfied with the image you create from your answers to Questions 14, 15, and 16, or if your choices raise your costs beyond your budget, modify them until you are pleased. Seek help if needed.

17. Describe the fears, resistances, or self-limiting patterns that you experienced while completing this activity. What are you ready to do about them?

18. Reflect on the important points in this activity and describe how you feel empowered.

19. In retrospect, what do you realize you already knew about planning and designing promotional materials?

20. What must you learn and develop? What resources are you ready to draw on? List in sequence the steps you will take and include dates, when appropriate.

◆

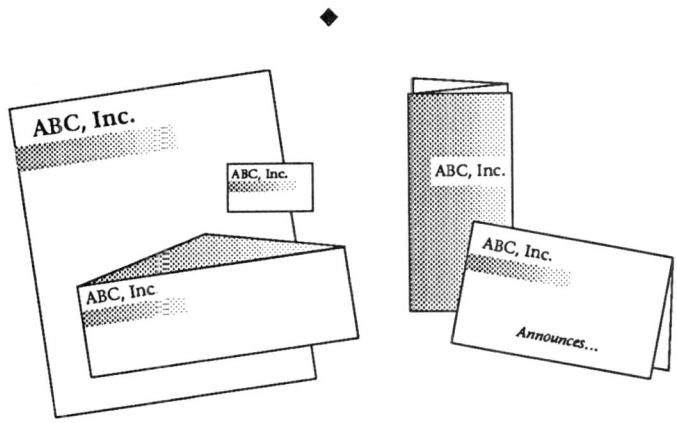

Financial Matters

Introduction

Note: Refer to the Glossary for definitions of unfamiliar words.

As you implement your promotion plan, and as your income and workload increase, you must manage the income you generate. This section on financial matters is intended to help you keep track of your income and develop the stability, security, and profit necessary to create the lifestyle you want. We are providing you with the simplest accounting system—the cash basis—designed in an easy-to-use format to help you maintain accurate records for management decisions, as well as for income tax purposes.

Many people resist keeping books and balancing bank statements because they believe these are overwhelming and difficult. They aren't, but if you don't want to keep track of your finances, contract with a bookkeeper or an accountant to do it for you. Before you do, study and understand this section so that you will know how to choose the right consultant for your needs. The cost will be small considering the care and protection a specialist will provide. You can minimize the fee by knowing the basics of accounting and by providing the appropriate information in an organized, efficient manner.

Financial management includes using your resources and assets to accomplish goals for stability and growth—through visioning, strategizing, and creating desired change. Accounting is the systematic approach to recording assets (resources), liabilities (debts), net worth, and the money you earn and spend. It includes financial statement preparation, break-even analysis, budgeting, tax preparation and filing, and being able to analyze and interpret the financial condition of your business at any time. Bookkeeping is the act of recording your financial transactions according to your accounting system's guidelines.

An accountant designs and sets up your financial systems and interprets your financial statements to give you advice. A CPA, or Certified Public Accountant, has been licensed by your state to certify that your financial statements have been prepared in accordance with generally accepted accounting principles. A bookkeeper maintains the daily activities of the system. The skills and duties of bookkeepers and accountants often overlap. (In this manual, we use the terms accountant and CPA interchangeably.) Request the names of bookkeepers, accountants, and CPAs from your mentors or others you trust. Interview several before making your choice. Your peace of mind and security result.

Cash accounting greatly simplifies your paperwork because you record income only when you receive it and expenses only as you pay them. With the accrual system, however, you record income when you agree to provide your service to a client, and expenses are recorded for the period in which they were incurred, regardless of when they are paid. An accrual system, therefore, includes both Accounts Receivable and Accounts Payable journals. In the interests of simplicity, this manual describes an accounting system based on the cash method.

Successful financial management requires an awareness of the various social and economic changes that may affect your income flow and stability. An effective manager is informed, flexible, adaptable, decisive, and ready to take action. Knowledge releases fear and helps to overcome resistance and inertia. As you learn about bookkeeping and accounting, your confidence and skills will grow, and your fear will dissipate. Remember, the number one accounting rule is: *Be consistent.* When you want to make changes in your accounting system, think them through, then proceed in an organized, consistent manner. Inconsistency creates confusion and errors. It also squanders energy and money.

In addition to providing a quality service, the primary objectives of your business are solvency and profitability, to provide income to the lifestyle you want. Unless you are able to produce adequate income, pay ongoing expenses, meet other obligations, and make a profit, your business will not survive, and you won't embody your vision or meet your objectives. Business is about providing a service and making money. With your business, you can create the lifestyle you want and enable others to do the same.

Many factors influence your choice of an accounting system. The system in this manual has been designed for a self-employed person—with no employees or inventory—who offers a service and receives payment when the service is rendered and who pays for goods and services when they are purchased. If your clients pay you over an extended period of time or if you make purchases on credit, you may want to use an accrual system. If you keep a folder for clients' occasional unpaid invoices and one for your unpaid expenses, you can easily determine what is owed to you—Accounts Receivable—and what you owe—Accounts Payable. If you need an accrual accounting system, consult your accountant. In addition, the organizational structure of your business—sole proprietorship, partnership, or corporation—may also affect the structure of your accounting system.

> *"Why do so many fail to become financially independent? I believe I have found the reasons. There are six, and here they are: (1) procrastination; (2) failure to establish a definite financial goal; (3) ignorance of what money must do to accomplish that goal; (4) failure to understand and apply our tax laws; (5) being sold the wrong kind of life insurance; and (6) failure to develop a winning mental attitude about money."*
> Venita Van Caspel

Basic Organizational Structures

Depending on your vision, service, and circumstances, one of the following basic organizational structures should be chosen for your business:

- Sole proprietorship
- Partnership
- Limited Liability Company
- Corporation
- S Corporation

Since this course is designed for individuals offering a service, the most appropriate organizational structure is probably a sole proprietorship. However, if you plan to expand, add partners, or find investors, a partnership or corporate structure may be more suitable. Our accounting system is designed for a sole proprietorship. However, your circumstances may call for a more complex bookkeeping procedure. With the guidance of your lawyer and accountant, choose the organizational structure and create the accounting system that best fulfills your needs.

A **sole proprietorship** is an unincorporated business owned and usually managed by one individual. Many services and small companies are organized as sole proprietorships. There are no legal formalities required, but depending on your service, you may need licensing, including trade name registration or sales tax licensing (see Appendix C). In a sole proprietorship, the owner takes sole responsibility for the debts of the business, pays taxes to the Internal Revenue Service (IRS) on a quarterly basis, and reports annual income using Schedule C, *Profit (or Loss) from Business or Profession*, and Schedule SE, *Computation of Social Security Self-Employment Tax*, which are included with his or her personal tax return. Personal assets are not protected in the event of business loss.

A **partnership** is a business owned and usually managed by two or more people. It should be created by a written partnership agreement, specifying the terms of the arrangement. The agreement should be thoroughly reviewed by an attorney for each partner. The agreement should detail the terms of the initial investments and the duties of each partner. It should clarify how income, profits, and losses are divided, as well as the process of settlement and termination in case either partner withdraws or dies. As with a sole proprietorship, there is no legal entity, and each partner pays quarterly taxes according to his or her proportionate shares of the partnership. As in sole proprietorships, partners expose their personal assets to liability and must file Form 1065, *U.S. Partnership Return of Income*, and Schedule SE with their federal tax returns.

The newest form of ownership is the **Limited Liability Company** (LLC). This organizational structure is currently authorized in a handful of states, but interest is growing in as many more. While neither a partnership nor a corporation, the LLC provides the benefits of both. LLCs do not pay taxes, nor are owners taxed on dividends, as with corporations. Each year owners can divide income and tax liablity as they see fit. With a minimum of two owners, LLCs protect owner's personal assets and do not limit their activities. Current drawbacks are several. IRS has thus far sanctioned the LLC structure only in Wyoming. It's not yet clear how LLCs will be governed when operating in states without LLC laws. Only Indiana recognizes LLCs organized elsewhere. There has been no litigation on LLCs so far, so no precedents have been set. To evaluate whether this option is right for you, see your attorney.

A **corporation** may be owned privately by one or more people, or publicly by thousands of people. Ownership is divided into shares of stock that are transferable through sale. Businesses are usually incorporated in the state where the business operates, but they can also be incorporated in other states for business and/or legal purposes. If incorporation out of state interests you, talk to your attorney. The corporation can be managed by the owners or by others. Major owners usually serve as officers. A corporation often evolves from a sole proprietorship or partnership once the business begins to require a broader range of expertise, or when the owners want to limit their personal liability for debt. Once a business is incorporated, owners are no longer self-employed, but receive income paid as wages, and have taxes withheld by the corporation. The corporation is the only organizational form that provides financial protection of owners' personal assets. As a legal entity, the corporation is required to file Form 1120, *U.S. Corporation Income Tax Return*.

An **S Corporation** combines some of the advantages of a corporation with some of the advantages of a sole proprietorship or a partnership. The number of stockholders is limited; they pay quarterly taxes and report income (or losses) on their personal income tax returns. In addition, the S corporation must file Form 1120S, *U.S. Income Tax Return for an S Corporation*, and the accompanying schedules.

See an attorney and/or an accountant to discuss the appropriate legal structure for your business and the circumstances that would require future changes. Explain the nature of your business, as well as your current and future goals. Most states provide an incorporation packet that, with a minimum registration fee, you can use to incorporate your business. It is worth a small fee to have an attorney or accountant review it.

Overview of an Accounting Strategy

An accounting strategy provides a systematic way to monitor and measure the financial health of your business. By keeping your books up to date and by preparing and reviewing financial statements regularly, you can make any necessary adjustments to ensure a long, healthy life for your business. In addition to maintaining your business as required by law, your accounting system will provide you with information to make the choices that support your needs and your vision.

The activities that follow (Activities 25-34) define accounting terms and teach you, step by step, how to set up and accurately maintain your financial management system. The following illustration should help you understand how the financial pieces fit together:

Section 3. Financial Matters

	ASSETS, LIABILITIES, NET WORTH	INCOME, EXPENSES
PROJECTED ON	Budget	Budget
RECORDED IN	Receipts & Disbursements Journals	Receipts & Disbursements Journals
SUMMARIZED IN	Receipts & Disbursements Summaries	Receipts & Disbursements Summaries
REPORTED ON	Balance Sheet	Profit & Loss Statement
ANALYZED WITH	Variance Statement	Variance Statement
RESULTING IN	Profitability, Stability	Solvency

To create your complete accounting strategy, follow these steps:

1. Clarify your vision, set goals, strategize, design plans, and set up systems to create stability and strength.

2. Create a budget. (Activities 25, Chart of Accounts, and 26, Budgeting.)

3. Record financial activities accurately, consistently, and regularly by using a simple bookkeeping system. (Activity 27, Receipts Journal, Activity 28, Disbursements Journal, and Activity 33, Petty Cash.)

4. Close your books at the end of each month and reconcile your bank statement. (Activity 27, Receipts Journal, Question 10; Activity 28, Disbursements Journal, Questions 9 and 11; and Activity 36, Balancing Your Bank Statement.)

5. Analyze and interpret financial information by creating a variance statement to compare the figures in your quarterly financial statements with the projected income and expenses from your budget. (Complete Activity 30, Variance Statement.)

6. If desired, prepare quarterly financial statements. (Complete Activity 29, Profit and Loss, and Activity 31, Balance Sheet.)

7. With your accountant's direction, prepare your estimated quarterly taxes. (See Taxes, Page 159.)

8. Prepare your annual financial statements and tax forms. (Complete Activities 29, and 30; and Taxes, Page 159.)

"Whatever you accept into your mind has reality for you.
It is your acceptance of it that makes it real."
Accept This Gift

Empowering Vision

Your Financial Map

Note: See Glossary for definitions.

The Chart of Accounts is the financial map of your accounting system, listing your business assets, liabilities, net worth, expenses, and income. The Master Chart of Accounts below is for a service business, operated by an individual without employees, and is based on the cash accounting system. For this reason, there are no accounts listed for salaries, payroll taxes, or inventory. If your business involves retail sales, manufacturing, or has employees, you will still benefit from studying accounting at this basic level. With the help of your accountant, you can incorporate the specific accounts you need into this Master Chart of Accounts.

Each of your financial transactions will fall into one of five major categories:

- Assets
- Liabilities
- Net Worth
- Income
- Expenses

Assets, liabilities, and net worth show what your business owns and owes—its solvency—as reflected on the Balance Sheet (Activity 31). Income and expenses show your income, expenses, and the resulting profitability, as outlined on the Profit and Loss Statement (Activity 29).

As you set up your books, you may find that you don't need as much detail as we show on the Master Chart of Accounts. Or, the nature of your service may require more detail than shown. For example, a person who has little outgoing mail and rarely needs copies may decide to combine copying, postage, and office supplies. Someone who frequently uses direct mail may want a detailed listing of postage to project marketing costs accurately. Feel free to add or delete accounts from the following lists.

Master Chart of Accounts

This Master Chart of Accounts serves as a blueprint for the activity that follows. Review the following accounts to begin determining the ones that apply to your business.

■ **ASSETS** *(from the most liquid—convertible to cash—to the least)*

Cash in Bank - Checking (account #)
Cash in Bank - Savings (account #)

Section 3. Financial Matters

Money Market Account (account #)
Petty Cash
Equipment
Furniture and Fixtures
Leasehold Improvements *(permanent changes you make to leased property for leases of more than one year; see your accountant for guidance)*

■ LIABILITIES

Loans Payable *(short-term - under a year)*
Notes Payable *(long-term - over a year)*

■ NET WORTH

Equity *(includes money and equipment you invest in your business and the profits you leave in the business)*
Draw *(amounts you take out of the business for your personal income - not an expense)*
Net Profit/(Loss)

■ INCOME

Program One
Program Two *(change these to short names of your programs)*
Program Three
<Refunds> *(entered as negative amounts because they reduce income)*
Interest *(received from savings or money market accounts)*
Service Charges *(fees you assess clients for late payment or for their checks returned by your bank)*
Miscellaneous

■ EXPENSES

Accounting and Legal
Advertising
Automobile Expenses *(gasoline, repairs, insurance)*
Bank Charges
Business or Trade Seminars
Contract Services *(for services performed by those who are not employees)*
Copying
Discounts *(difference between regular fee and what you actually charge a client (Activity 27))*
Dues, Subscriptions, Memberships
Entertainment
Equipment Leasing and Rental
Fees and Licenses
Insurance *(fire, theft, liability, as appropriate)*
Interest *(paid on business loans and credit cards)*
Laundry
Miscellaneous
Office Supplies *(may include copying and postage)*
Other Supplies *(specify)*
Postage

Empowering Vision

Printing
Promotion *(various promotional fees, networking costs; may include ads and promotional materials)*
Promotional Materials *(graphics, editing, typesetting, printing, or each may be listed separately)*
Rent
Repairs and Maintenance of Property and Equipment *(may include janitorial)*
Sales Commissions
Taxes
Telephone
Travel
Utilities

Note: If you have depreciable assets (furniture, equipment, vehicle), your accountant will advise you on the best way to determine depreciation. However, because depreciation is not an expense in the cash accounting system, it is not included in this Chart of Accounts.

> *"If you have built castles in the air,
> your work need not be lost.
> That is where they should be.
> Now put the foundations under them."*
> Henry David Thoreau

 Activity 25. Chart of Accounts

1. Review Activity 5, Organizing Your Business, Questions 7 and 9; and Activity 11, Program Planning and Development, Question 11, to evaluate the types of expenses you will routinely encounter in your business.

2. Create your Chart of Accounts by following the instructions in a-e below, and by making a list of all the account categories for your business. In addition, for all assets, liabilities, and equity in a, b, and c below, you will establish your initial balances—the amount of cash owned and debt owed by your business when the accounting system is begun.

    a. Under Assets, list everything your business owns. First, list each business account that is either cash or is an item that can be sold and thus converted to cash. List the current amount of cash in each business account: checking, savings, money market funds, petty cash, stocks or bonds. List items your business owns and the original price paid for each: furniture, equipment, land, vehicles. List any other assets, including major improvements you have made to property you lease.

    Note: If you have brought personal assets, including cash, into your business, ask your accountant to help you establish their value. Include under c below.

b. Under Liabilities, list what your business owes. Include short-term loans and long-term notes. List each separately, including the amounts owed for each.

c. Under Net Worth, indicate Equity—the amount of money or equipment you or others have invested in your business. See your accountant to determine these amounts. Add Draw to your list—the category on your Chart of Accounts under which you will record the cash you draw for personal income. This is not an expense, but rather a reduction in the value or net worth of your business. Net Profit or Loss is where the profit or loss of your business is recorded. It is calculated by preparing a Profit and Loss Statement (Activity 29).

d. Under Income, refer to Activity 5, Question 9, and list all your sources of income. Include income from all your programs, interest on business savings or money market accounts, and service charges assessed your clients. Use Miscellaneous Income for other types of income that occur irregularly. Add other income categories that are not included here.

e. Under Expenses, refer to Activity 5, Questions 7 and 9; Activity 11, Question 11; and Activity 21, Question 8, and list the types of expenses you expect. Evaluate the Master Chart of Accounts on Pages 122-124 to add additional expense categories to your list. If you have operated this business previously, analyze your prior financial data from Schedule C, Profit or Loss from Business or Profession, filed with last year's tax return. If you have no historical data, estimate expenses for each of your programs by using prior utility, telephone, and other bills.

As previously indicated, use as much or as little detail as is appropriate for your type of business and extent of business management you choose to maintain.

Note: If you work in your home, you may be able to claim certain expenses as deductions. Ask your accountant.

Make all financial management decisions based on what you sincerely believe empowers your vision and goals. If you want to strengthen your financial management skills, create a detailed Chart of Accounts. If you never plan to use a budget, keep your details simple.

3. When complete, review and evaluate your Chart of Accounts. Within each category, arrange Assets, Liabilities, Net Worth, and Income items as illustrated on our Master Chart of Accounts, and arrange expense items alphabetically.

4. Keep your Chart of Accounts handy as you complete the remaining activities in this section.

5. After you have worked with your new accounting system for several months, you may choose to revise your Chart of Accounts. You may want to expand or consolidate certain categories or perhaps add or remove assets bought or sold, and liabilities incurred or paid. Make these

Empowering Vision

revisions before you begin a new statement period. If you have any questions, ask your accountant for help.

6. Recall and describe the fears, resistances, or self-limiting patterns that you experienced while completing this activity. List them in order of priority and explain what you will do about them.

7. Reflect on the important points this activity revealed to you and describe how you feel empowered. How will this affect your ability to reach and attract the clients you choose?

8. What do you need to learn? What are the steps you will take? Include dates, when appropriate.

◆

Business is like a game of strategy. Learn the principles, rules, and the moves, do your best, and enjoy.

Section 3. Financial Matters

Budgeting

A budget is a projection of income and expenses for a specific project or a determined period of time. Expenses include basic business overhead and program expenses—the costs you expect to incur to implement your income-generating program(s). You have already created the foundation for your budget by using this activity to complete Questions 7 and 9 in Activity 5, Organizing Your Business, in regard to overhead and start-up costs; Question 11 in Activity 11, Program Planning and Development, about program income and expenses; and Activity 32, Break-even point calculation. Now you can review your figures and organize them into a formal budget.

Your budget answers two basic questions: What personal income do I want to earn from each program; and what will it cost me to earn this income? Budgeting is an essential management process because it allows you to utilize and allocate your resources to generate income.

Because you are self-employed or are considering self-employment, it is essential to project the income necessary to satisfy both the costs of doing business and of providing your personal income. If you are already self-employed, do not spend another dime for marketing, new equipment, or education until you use this activity to prepare a monthly budget for the next financial period. This is essential if you want to manage your money effectively.

If desired, you may prepare a budget for basic overhead and one for each of your programs, then combine them into one budget for a specific period. In this way, you will gain control over your cash flow by knowing where it is coming from and where it is going. The best way to make sound financial decisions is to create a budget and follow it. Use pencil and a good eraser so your budget is easy to read. You will need the following materials:

- 13-column, 41-line, 11 x 16-3/8 columnar pad, lines on one side only

Sheets are punched for binder storage, or you can use a file folder. (They can be folded to fit either.)

As you prepare your budget, you will notice that you might not have all the figures you need. When this happens, use your intuition or even guess, then refer to prior periods and do the research necessary to determine the more accurate figure.

When you record the more accurate figure, compare it with your estimate. How close were you? This is a valuable step in learning how to estimate costs. Remember that your budget is only an estimate of income and expenses to help you manage your resources and fulfill your goals.

As a planning and financial-control tool, your budget should include:

- All categories of expected income and expenses that result from planned activities and projects

- Fixed and variable operating expenses such as rent, utilities, and phone

- Expenses that have been incurred in prior periods but are not yet paid in full (outstanding invoices or debts).

✍ Activity 26. The Budgeting Process

1. **Initial Review and Evaluation.** Your budget should be:

    a. The reflection of the specific requirements of your vision, purpose, goals, objectives, and current financial requirements. Referring to Activity 5, Organizing Your Business, Questions 7 and 9, summarize specific items that you need to start or enhance your business. Research their costs and arrange them in order of priority.

    b. A realistic projection of your ongoing activities and your regular, periodic, and one-time projects. List the title of each income-generating program.

    c. A carefully prepared monitoring tool. Review your research from Activities 5 and 11, and evaluate your needs and priorities:

        1) Consider the level of detail you need and are willing to use. Keeping it simple makes it easier and more fun. How much detail are you willing to work with? (For example, a massage therapist needs to estimate the amount of laundry soap needed, but calculating the exact amount of soap needed for each load is too much detail. Instead, the cost should be determined by the average number of boxes purchased in a month.)

        2) Determine the time frame for your budget. If you feel you need to develop confidence with the budgeting process, you may begin by projecting for only one month at a time. This way, you can compare your budgeted amounts with your actual income and expenses and adjust the next month's budget accordingly. To do this, use Activity 30, Variance Statement. Eventually, you will easily be able to project for each financial period and even for a year.

        3) Review current social and economic conditions and trends in your community. What is the probable availability of disposable income for the service you provide? Talk with an accountant to learn about any changes in tax laws that might affect your decision-making and tax liability.

        4) Evaluate your priorities, programs, and general activities to determine if any changes are needed. Do you still choose to implement these programs according to your original plans?

        5) Complete Activity 25, Chart of Accounts.

Section 3. Financial Matters

2. **Budget Preparation.** Study the Sample Budget on Page 132 as you read through the rest of this activity. Make notes as appropriate. Use the Sample Budget format for your budget, adapting it to include the level of detail and specific categories you require.

   On 13-column paper, using pencil, fill in each month's figures, following the Sample Budget.

   a. Time Period. Determine the period of time for this budget.

   b. Income. From your Chart of Accounts, Activity 25, and Program Planning and Development, Activity 11, Question 11, list the income categories and projected income from each, beginning with those that provide the greatest income. Total the income figures. Write short or abbreviated names for your programs, and leave several blank spaces at the end of the list for additions.

      1) Review your list to check that you:

         a) Were realistic and conservative with income projections. When in doubt, underestimate income

         b) Evaluated the impact of potential economic, legal, social, and political trends on your income

         c) Evaluated seasonal fluctuations in income for your service.

      2) Make adjustments as necessary and total again.

   c. Expenses. From your Chart of Accounts, and from Activity 5, Organizing Your Business, Questions 7 and 9, and Activity 11, Program Planning and Development, Question 11, list the projected expenses for your time period. Add any that are not listed. Organize them in alphabetical order and total. Review your expenses from prior periods for assistance. Leave several blank lines for additions.

      1) Review the expenses you listed to be certain that you:

         a) Were realistic, liberal, and flexible with projections. When in doubt, overestimate expenses

         b) Evaluated the impact of potential economic, legal, social, and political trends. Consider seasonal fluctuations of expenses and projected projects

         c) Included taxes as an expense, estimated at about 20 percent of your total income for income and self-employment taxes. If applicable, also include estimates for sales and personal property taxes

         d) Built a cushion into your budget by adding 10 percent of your total expenses for miscellaneous or unforeseen expenses that periodically occur.

2) Consider asking a successful, non-competitive individual who offers the same service to help you determine which expenses are necessary and which are not. Ask for help determining whether these costs will provide a worthwhile return. Add any new categories to your Chart of Accounts.

d. Net Profit. Total your expenses, then subtract this figure from your income total. If expenses are higher than income, you have projected a loss and will need to increase your income, decrease expenses, or both. You need enough profit to meet your personal income goals and provide the lifestyle you want.

Consider whether your fees are adequate for your service. (Activity 13, Fees, Dicounts & Collections) If not, re-evaluate your priorities and make appropriate changes. If you must decrease expenses, begin with the frills.

3. **Using Your Budget.**

    a. Use your budget—review and evaluate it regularly. Use the Variance Statement (Activity 30) to compare budget projections with actual amounts. When you calculate your quarterly financial statements, using Activity 29, Profit and Loss Statement, and Activity 30, Variance Statement, you will determine whether you have accurately projected your cash flow by comparing your financial statement with budget projections.

    b. You will make changes in your budget as your needs, income, and programs change. Prepare a new budget each time you create a new vision and set new and different goals. It is best to revision, plan, and develop strategies twice yearly to keep up with personal, social, and economic changes. Stability and success require management. Remember, management really can be fun!

    Note: Keep your budgeting notes for future reference. You will need them for budget revisions and reviews, as well as for next year's budget.

    > *"The secret of success*
    > *is to be ready for opportunity*
    > *when it comes."*
    > Disraeli

4. **So, how did it go?**

    a. Recall and describe the fears, resistances, or self-limiting patterns you experienced while completing this activity. List them in order of priority and explain what you are ready to do about them.

    b. What fears or resistances were you able to release? Explain.

c. Reflect on the important points this activity revealed to you and describe how you feel empowered.

d. In retrospect, what have you realized that you already knew about budgeting?

e. What must you learn and develop as a business manager? What resources are you ready to draw on? How can your mentors help you? List the steps you will take and include dates, when appropriate.

◆

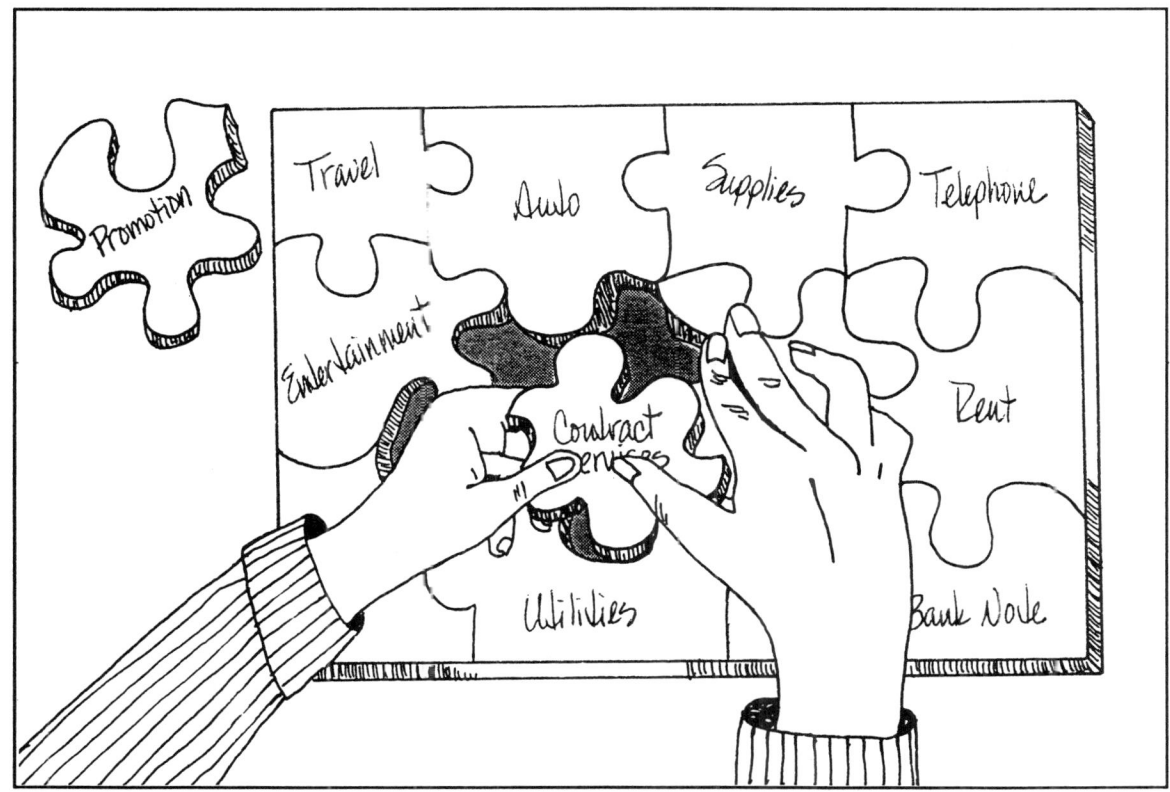

Creating a budget enables you to clearly see your financial picture and make informed decisions.

Empowering Vision

Sample Budget Worksheet

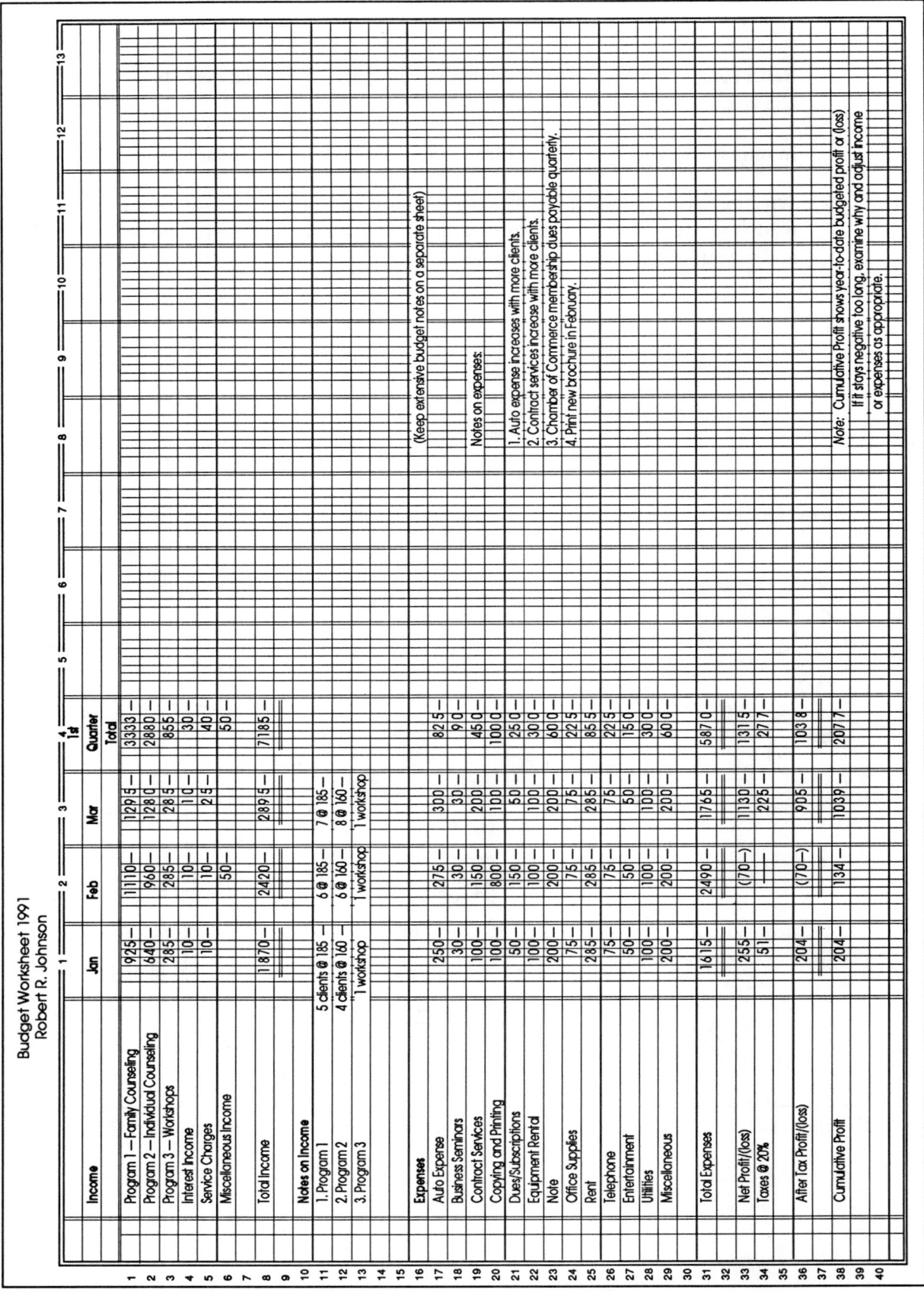

Budget Worksheet 1991
Robert R. Johnson

Income	Jan	Feb	Mar	1st Quarter Total
Program 1 — Family Counseling	925 —	1110 —	1295 —	3330 —
Program 2 — Individual Counseling	640 —	960 —	1280 —	2880 —
Program 3 — Workshops	285 —	285 —	285 —	855 —
Interest Income	10 —	10 —	10 —	30 —
Service Charges	10 —		25 —	40 —
Miscellaneous Income		50 —		50 —
Total Income	1870 —	2420 —	2895 —	7185 —
Notes on Income				
1. Program 1	5 clients @ 185	6 @ 185	7 @ 185	
2. Program 2	4 clients @ 160	6 @ 160	8 @ 160	
3. Program 3	1 workshop	1 workshop	1 workshop	
				(Keep extensive budget notes on a separate sheet)
Expenses				
Auto Expense	250 —	275 —	300 —	825 —	Notes on expenses:
Business Seminars	30 —	30 —	30 —	90 —
Contract Services	100 —	150 —	200 —	450 —	1. Auto expense increases with more clients.
Copying and Printing	100 —	800 —	100 —	1000 —	2. Contract services increase with more clients.
Dues/Subscriptions	50 —	150 —	50 —	250 —	3. Chamber of Commerce membership dues payable quarterly.
Equipment Rental	100 —	100 —	100 —	300 —	4. Print new brochure in February.
Note	200 —	200 —	200 —	600 —
Office Supplies	75 —	75 —	75 —	225 —
Rent	285 —	285 —	285 —	855 —
Telephone	75 —	75 —	75 —	225 —
Entertainment	50 —	50 —	50 —	150 —
Utilities	100 —	100 —	100 —	300 —
Miscellaneous	200 —	200 —	200 —	600 —
Total Expenses	1615 —	2490 —	1765 —	5870 —
Net Profit/(loss)	255 —	(70 —)	1130 —	1315 —
Taxes @ 20%	51 —		225 —	277 —
After Tax Profit/(loss)	204 —	(70 —)	905 —	1038 —
Cumulative Profit	204 —	134 —	1039 —	2077 —

Note: Cumulative Profit shows year-to-date budgeted profit or (loss). If it stays negative too long, examine why and adjust income or expenses as appropriate.

A Simple Bookkeeping System

The purpose of your bookkeeping system is to track accurately the cash flow of your business, to know the sources of income and the nature of expenses. When your records agree with your bank's records, you know your exact profit and the amount of taxes you must pay.

Using your Chart of Accounts (Activity 25), your Budget (Activity 26), and the Receipts and the Disbursements Journals that follow as guides, you can create your bookkeeping system to provide the detail you want. Begin both journals on the first day of your accounting period on January 1 or on the day of the first income or expense transaction in the month you begin your business. Use pencil and a good eraser so your books are easy to read. You will need the following materials:

- 6-column, 41-line, 8-1/2 x 11 columnar pad
- 13-column, 41-line, 11 x 16-3/8 columnar pad, lines on one side only

Both sheets should be punched for binder storage, or you can use a file folder. The 13-column sheets can be folded to fit either.

Activity 27. Receipts Journal

Your Receipts Journal is a record of the source and amounts of all income. These include payments from clients, interest on business savings or money market accounts, service charges assessed clients, and refunds for services. Maintain a separate Receipts Journal for each bank account used for business transactions. As you complete this activity, refer to each of the samples on Pages 134, 137, and 139.

1. **Labeling the Journal Page.**

    a. Carefully study the Receipts Journal Sample, Page 134.

    b. Title a 6-column journal page with the name listed on your checking account, along with "Receipts Journal" and your account number.

    c. Label the two left columns "Date" and "Source."

    d. In the first numerical column—column 1—write "Cash." This column corresponds to "Assets—Cash in Bank—Checking" on your Chart of Accounts. Entries in this column increase your cash.

    e. In columns 2, 3, and 4, write the names of your income-generating programs, beginning with the most active in column 2 to the least active in column 4.

Empowering Vision

Sample Receipts Journal

Receipts Journal
Account #485621

1991 Date	Source	Cash	Program 1 Family Counseling	Program 2 Individual Counseling	Program 3 Workshops	Miscellaneous Expl.	Amount
Jan 6	Blackstock	185 —	185 —				
7	Larsen	160 —		160 —			
8	Carroll	185 —	185 —				
8	ABC Office Supply	9 75				Office Supply Reimbursement	9 75
10	Morris	185 —	185 —				
13	Mishabek	185 —	185 —				
13	Hirsch	160 —		160 —			
17	Smith	160 —		160 —			
19	ABC Office Supply	20 27				Office Supply Reimbursement	20 27
20	Murray	345 —	185 —	160 —			
21	Bloomfield	160 —		160 —			
21	Romney	185 —	185 —				
22	Smith (check return)	<160 —>		<160 —>			
23	First Bank	200 —				Telephone Transfer from savings	200 —
24	Arnold	185 —	185 —				
27	Simmons	185 —	185 —				
27	Jones	140 —		140 —			
28	Burr	185 —	185 —				
29	Freeman	185 —	185 —				
30	Miller	170 —		160 —		Service Charge	10 —
31	B.O.E.A.	285 —			285 —		
31	First Bank	6 85				Interest	6 85
	January Total	3321 87	1850 —	940 —	285 —		246 87

Miscellaneous Summary:

Office Supply Reimbursement	30 02
Transfer from Savings	200 —
Interest	6 85
Service Charge	10 —
	246 87

f. Columns 5 and 6, as you can see from the Receipts Journal Sample, are for miscellaneous and periodic kinds of income, such as interest and service fees. Write "Miscellaneous" across both columns, then "Expl." (explanation) on the left and "Amount" on the right underneath.

2. **Making Entries.**

   a. Record all the checks you receive in your Receipts Journal when you prepare to make your bank deposit. Always make sure the total you record in your journal and the total of the deposit agree.

   b. Deposit all business earnings into this account, and record all amounts received in your Receipts Journal. Also, for simplicity, do not ask for cash back from business deposits. Instead, write yourself a check and record it as a draw. For the times when you need cash for small business purchases, create a Petty Cash system. (See Activity 33.)

   > *"Faith is the starting point of all accumulation of riches!*
   > *Have faith in yourself; faith in the Infinite."*
   > Napoleon Hill

   c. To make an entry in your Receipts Journal, write the date on which you received payment in the Date column and record your client's last name in the Source column. (If payment is by check, include the name that appears on the check.) The column is small, so abbreviate as needed.

   d. Write the full amount of the check in the Cash column, and write the amount again under the appropriate program (columns 2-4) or Miscellaneous, column 6, and include a brief explanation of the source.

   If you receive one payment for two or more programs, write the full amount under Cash, then distribute the appropriate amounts to the various programs. (See Receipts Journal Sample, line 10.) Be careful—this is when errors may occur. If part of a client's payment is for a service charge (for late payment or a returned check), enter the service charge portion in the Miscellaneous column. (See line 20, Receipts Journal Sample.)

3. **Reversing an Entry.** If a client's check is returned for insufficient funds, list it as a reversal in your Receipts Journal in the appropriate program column by bracketing the amount, <160.00>, and entering the date that the bank deducted it from your account. (See line 13 on Receipts Journal Sample.) If there are bank charges, you will record them in your Disbursements Journal when you reconcile your bank statement (Activity 34).

4. **Reimbursements.** If you receive a reimbursement from a supplier, it will reduce the amount of the expense. However, this amount is recorded and explained in your Receipts Journal in the Miscellaneous column. Then, when you prepare your Profit and Loss Statement, the amount

Empowering Vision

will be subtracted from the proper expense category. (See lines 4 and 9 on Receipts Journal Sample.)

Note: When you write a refund check to a client, it is not an expense, but a reduction in your income. However, you will record it in the Miscellaneous column of your Disbursements Journal (See Activity 28, Question 4). Later, you will transfer the total amount refunded to the refund line in the Income section of your Profit and Loss Statement (See Activity 29, Profit and Loss Statement).

5. **Discounts.** If you offer your services at a discount, add a 6-column sheet to your bookkeeping system and title it "Discount Schedule." After studying Discount Schedule Sample, label column 1 "Full Price," column 2 "Discount," column 3 "Amount Received," and columns 4 and 5 "Explanation." Record it each time you offer your service at a discount. Total at the end of each month, quarter, and year. Your accountant will use your Discount Schedule to determine the portion of discounts that can be deducted from your gross income.

6. **Bank Credits.** Each month, after you have balanced your bank statement, record in your Receipts Journal any interest earned and any bank credit memos. (See line 22, Receipts Journal Sample.)

7. **Totals.** Skip a line after the last entry, write Total in the Source column, then total each column. Double underscore each total. (See line 24, Receipts Journal Sample.)

8. **Check Math.** This is a double-entry system, so you can easily verify that your calculations are correct by adding the totals of columns 2, 3, 4, and 6. These should equal the total of column 1, Cash. The equation is $2 + 3 + 4 + 6 = 1$.

   If possible, use a calculator with a tape printout. If you find you have made an error, compare the tape with the amounts in the columns. If correct, verify line by line that the total of columns 2, 3, 4, and 6 equals column 1.

9. **Monthly Miscellaneous Receipts Summary.** Create a monthly summary of the income listed in the Miscellaneous column if there are more than two entries for one category. (See lines 30-37, Receipts Journal Sample.) Make sure your total agrees with the total of the Miscellaneous column.

10. **Receipts Summary.** Create a Receipts Summary on 13-column paper to provide quarterly and year-end income totals. (See Receipts Summary Sample.)

    a. In the Source column, list each month; total every three months for the quarterly total; and calculate the year-to-date subtotal (YTD) after the second and third quarter subtotals. End with the annual totals. Double underscore all totals.

    b. Each month, transfer the totals from columns 2-4 on the Receipts Journal to the corresponding columns 2-4 on the Receipts Summary. Use columns 5-13 on the

Section 3. Financial Matters

Sample Discount Schedule

Discount Schedule
1991

1991 Date	Source	Full Price	Discount	Amt. Received	Explanation
1 27	Jones	160 —	20 —	140 —	low income client
2 15	Jones	160 —	20 —	140 —	low income client
3 7	Peters	160 —	20 —	140 —	low income client
3 28	Jones	160 —	20 —	140 —	low income client
	March Total	320 —	40 —	280 —	
	1st Quarter	640 —	80 —	560 —	

Note: If only one line is entered during a month, double underscore the amounts to indicate the total.

Receipts Summary to list all miscellaneous income categories from the Miscellaneous Summaries in your Receipts Journal. Then, transfer the amounts from the Journal Miscellaneous Summaries to the appropriate column on your Receipts Summary.

c. Compute totals for each quarter and double underscore the quarterly totals. Add the new quarter total to the previous quarter(s) total to get the year-to-date total. At the end of the year, skip a few lines and add the quarterly totals to obtain annual totals, and double underscore. Transfer quarterly and annual totals to the Profit and Loss Statement (Activity 29) and Balance Sheet (Activity 31), as appropriate. Study the Notes on Receipts Summary Sample (lines 32-37, Page 139).

11. **So, how did it go?**

a. Recall and describe the fears, resistances, or self-limiting patterns you experienced while completing this activity. List them in order of priority and explain what you are ready to do about them.

b. What fears or resistances were you able to release? Explain.

c. Reflect on the important points this activity revealed to you and describe how you feel empowered.

d. In retrospect, what have you realized that you already knew about a receipts journal?

e. What must you learn and develop as a business manager? What resources are you ready to draw on? How can your mentors help you? List the steps you will take and include dates, when appropriate.

◆

*"If one advances confidently
in the direction of his dreams,
and endeavors to live the life
which he has imagined,
he will meet with a success
unexpected in common hours."*
Thoreau

Section 3. Financial Matters

Sample Receipts Summary

Robert R. Johnson
Receipts Summary 1991

	Total	Program 1 Family Counseling	Program 2 Individual Counseling	Program 3 Workshops	Interest	Transfer from Savings	Office Supply Reimburs.	Service Charges
January	3321 87	1850 —	940 —	285 —	685	200 —	3002	10 —
February	3082 50	1850 —	940 —	285 —	750	—	—	—
March	3380 46	2035 —	940 —	285 —	796	100 —	1250	10 —
1st Quarter	9784 83	5735 —	2820 —	855 —	2231	300 —	4252	10 —
April	3573 50	2025 —	960 —	570 —	850	—	—	—
May	3794 11	2035 —	960 —	570 —	911	200 —	10261	20 —
June	4022 33	2220 —	1120 —	570 —	972	—	—	—
2nd Quarter	11389 94	6290 —	3040 —	1710 —	2733	200 —	10261	20 —
Year-to-date	21174 77	12025 —	5860 —	2565 —	4964	500 —	14513	30 —
July	4055 01	2220 —	960 —	855 —	1001	—	—	10 —
August	4205 77	2220 —	1120 —	855 —	1077	—	—	—
September	4226 51	2220 —	1120 —	855 —	1151	—	—	20 —
3rd Quarter	12487 29	6660 —	3200 —	2565 —	3229	—	—	30 —
Year-to-date	33652 06	18685 —	9060 —	5130 —	8193	500 —	14513	60 —
October	4492 10	2220 —	1120 —	1140 —	1210	—	22 —	—
November	4515 42	2220 —	1120 —	1140 —	1342	—	—	—
December	4494 —	2220 —	1120 —	1140 —	14 —	—	—	—
4th quarter	13501 52	6660 —	3360 —	3420 —	3952	—	22 —	—
1987 Totals	47163 58	25345 —	12420 —	8550 —	12142	500 —	16713	60 —

Notes on how to transfer totals to financial statements:

- Transfer Program Income to your Profit and Loss Statement under "Program Income."
- Transfer Interest to Profit & Loss Statement under "Interest Income."
- Transfer to Balance Sheet, reducing "Savings Acct." and increasing "Cash on Hand Expense."
- Transfer to Profit & Loss Statement, reducing "Office Supply Expense."
- Transfer to Profit & Loss Statement, "Service Charges."

Add 2nd Quarter figures to 1st Quarter to get year-to-date

Add 3rd Quarter to previous year-to-date figures to get new year-to-date

Add 4th Quarter to previous year-to-date figures to get annual totals.

Empowering Vision

✍ Activity 28. Disbursements Journal

The Disbursements Journal, similar in design to the Receipts Journal, is used to record all decreases in cash: expenses, the purchase of assets, leasehold improvements, bank charges, and personal draws. If you have a savings or money market account from which you make regular withdrawals, you will need a separate Disbursements Journal for each account. Begin your Disbursements Journal on the same date that you began your Receipts Journal. Use pencil. While completing this activity, refer to Disbursements Journal Sample on Page 141 and Disbursements Summary Sample on Page 143.

Note: If you don't like doing your books, but still choose to do them yourself, keep them simple. If you don't like doing them and want lots of detail, consider paying someone else to do them.

1. **Chart of Accounts.**

    a. Review the categories of expenses you finalized from Activity 25, Chart of Accounts.

    b. Evaluate these categories to determine the level of detail you want. Using "Promotion" as an illustration, you may prefer to include advertising as a cost of promotion. Or, you may want to know exactly what you pay for advertising, distinct from all other promotional costs.

    c. Choose the expense categories appropriate for your management needs.

2. **Labeling the Page.**

    a. Carefully study the Disbursements Journal Sample.

    b. As with the Receipts Journal, write your business name, "Disbursements Journal," and account number at the top of a sheet of 13-column paper.

    c. In the first two left-hand columns, write "Date" and "Payee." In column 1 write "Check No.," and in column 2 write "Cash." If you intend to use this account for personal as well as business expenses, write "Draw" in column 11 and "Miscellaneous" on the top line across columns 12 and 13, identifying 12 as "Expl." and 13 as "Amount" on the center line.

    d. Evaluate your Budget (Activity 26) to determine the frequency of purchases and projected expenses. Number this list from the most used to the least, so that the most used columns on your Disbursements Journal will be closest to column 2. (You may need to guess or use intuition. You can always rearrange them in the next financial statement period.)

    e. Write these expense categories in order of most used, from left to right, using columns 3-10.

Section 3. Financial Matters

Sample Disbursements Journal

Robert R. Johnson
Disbursements Journal   Acct. # 485621

	1991 Date	Payee	1 Check No.	2 Cash	3 Entertainment	4 Advertising	5 Auto Expenses	6 Contract Services	7 Dues, Subs, Membership	8 Office Supplies	9 Copying & Printing	10 Note	11 Draw	12 Miscellaneous Expl.	13 Amount
1	Jan 1	Florence Roberts	3456	285—										Rent	285—
2	1	Chevron U.S.A.	3457	26 81			26 81								
3	1	Daily Tribune	3458	48 22		48 22									
4	1	Cash	3459	50—										Petty Cash	50—
5	1	Peter King	3460	60—				60—							
6	1	Local Bell	3461	68 75										Telephone	68 75
7	1	Farmer's Insurance	3462	387 82			387 82								
8	6	Psychology Today	3463	40—					40—						
9	8	Rental City	3464	54—										Equip. Rental	54—
10	8	J. Larsen	3465	40—										Partial Refund	40—
11	10	Autsy Copy	3466	23 02							23 02				
12	13	John's Restaurant	3467	43 38	43 38										
13	15	Postmaster	3468	22—										Postage	22—
14	15	Robert R. Johnson	3469	350—									350—		
15	15	Texaco	3470	34 89			34 89								
16	15	Chamber of Commerce	3471	50—					50—						
17	15	ABC Office Supply	3472	26 84						26 84					
18	15	Nexus	3473	75—			75—								
19	15	First Bank	3474	189 16								166 47		Interest	22 69
20	15	VISA	3475	162—	78 21		67 78			16 01					
21	20	Career Track	3476	90—										Seminar	90—
22	21	Camilla Sanford	3477	48—				48—							
23	24	Robert R. Johnson	3478	350—									350—		
24	29	Cash	3479	47 55	11 50					10 85				Misc.	3 20
25	30	First Bank	—	2 71										Postage	22—
														Bank Charges	2 71
28		January Total		2525 14	133 09	123 22	467 30	108—	90—	53 70	23 02	166 47	700—		660 34

Miscellaneous Summary:
Rent	285—
Petty Cash	50—
Telephone	68 75
Equip. Rental	54—
Refund Client	40—
Postage	44—
Interest	22 69
Bus. Seminar	90—
Bank Charges	2 71
Misc.	3 20
	660 34

Empowering Vision

3. **Making Entries.**

    a. To make an entry in your Disbursements Journal, write the date of the check in the Date column. Write the name on the check in the Payee column and the check number in column 1. Abbreviate when needed.

    b. Write the amount of the check in column 2, "Cash." Determine the expense category and write the amount in the appropriate column. If you write a check for more than one expense, write the total in the Cash column and disburse the expense carefully into the appropriate categories. (See check #3475 on line 20, Disbursements Journal Sample.)

    c. File the receipt, invoice, or other source document, marked with the check number, date paid, and amount, in the appropriate file. (See Activity 15, Filing System.)

4. **Refunds.** If you write a refund check to a client, record it in the Miscellaneous column in your Disbursements Journal as a refund. (See line 10, Disbursements Sample.) You will transfer it to your Profit and Loss Statement as a reversal in the income section, which will reduce your gross income. (See Activity 29, Profit and Loss Statement.)

5. **Bank charges.** At the end of each month, record in your Disbursements Journal and in your checkbook register any bank charges or debits. These may include automatic deductions or cash withdrawals from automatic banking machines, or debit card purchases. (See line 25, Disbursements Journal Sample.)

6. **Totals.** Skip a line after your last entry, and total all columns as you did for Receipts. Double underscore the totals.

7. **Check math.** Verify that your math is correct, using this formula: column 2 = the sum of columns 3 through 11, plus 13.

8. **Miscellaneous Summary.** Create a monthly summary of miscellaneous expenses as you did for Receipts by listing each different item in column 12 and entering the total for that category next to it. Place this summary in the lower right corner of the page, as shown on Disbursements Journal Sample. Make sure your total agrees with the total of the Miscellaneous column.

9. **Disbursements Summary.** Create a Disbursements Summary on 13-column paper to provide quarterly and year-end expense totals. (See Disbursements Summary Sample, Page 143.)

    a. Write the months at the top of columns 1-12; label column 13 "Total." List your expense categories alphabetically down the left side. Include all categories from your miscellaneous summaries.

    b. Each month, transfer the totals from your Disbursements Journal to the Disbursements Summary. Because there is not enough space on this Summary to calculate

Section 3. Financial Matters

Sample Disbursements Summary

Robert R. Johnson
Disbursements Summary 1991

	Jan	Feb	Mar	Apr	May	Jun	Jul	Aug	Sep	Oct	Nov	Dec	Total
Accounting & Legal		150 —				200 —	550 —			150 —			1050 —
Advertising	1232 2	1485 7	9812	1450 —	12786	1450	9826	18512	7540	14500	12987	26411	429567
Auto Expense	46730	27583	29612	31974	22533	31286	55219	29683	37504	31222	38419	3255	419267
Bank Charges	271	453	291	1840	350	612	419	502	623	724	314	222	6626
Business Seminars	90 —				90 —				90 —				270 —
*Cash – Savings Account		200 —				400 —		400 —		600 —		600 —	2200 —
Contract Services	108 —	150 —	175 —	175 —	150 —	108 —	150 —	175 —	175 —	175 —	175 —	200 —	1916 —
Copying & Printing	2502	14779	85 —	5462	2304	5490	2517	4627	8514	4620	11740	20 —	195976
*Draw	700 —	700 —	700 —	2000 —	2500 —	2500 —	2500 —	2700 —	3000 —	3000 —	3000 —	3200 —	26700 —
Dues, Subs, Membership	90 —			75 —		120 —			55 —		75 —		415 —
*Equipment			254319				215712						470031
Equip. Lease & Rental	54 —	54 —	54 —	54 —	54 —	54 —							324 —
Fees & Licenses							75 —						75 —
Furniture & Fixtures								115097					115097
Interest Expense	2269	2150	2099	1947	11901	11857	11799	11722	1685	1601	15430	1444	220017
*Leasehold Improvements						135 —							135 —
Miscellaneous	320		275					418					1017
*Money Market Act.			100 —		100 —		100 —		100 —		200 —		600 —
Notes	16647	16766	16817	16964	17015	17059	17117	17194	17231	17318	17373	17472	204975
Office Supplies	5370	6210	4819	3691	5420	3711	4326	5740	3211	1940	3652	4791	52881
*Petty Cash	50 —												50 —
Postage	44 —	38 —	22 —	44 —	17 —	39 —	44 —	2760	44 —	39 —	14 —		37360
Promotion		250 —			250 —			250 —			380 —		1080 —
*Refunds	40 —					30 —				10 —			80 —
Rent	285 —	285 —	285 —	285 —	285 —	285 —	285 —	285 —	285 —	285 —	285 —	285 —	3420 —
Telephone	6874	6874	6874	9320	6874	8211	6874	7326	7412	6874	7319	6874	87706
Entertainment	15309	15619	15522	5312	6410	1943	2875	45622	8540	3210	1911	24375	144648
Utilities			7840			8310			9640			4320	30110
Total Disbursements	252514	421212	490386	484815	425193	480079	707084	630203	4768	638406	493163	548909	6048764

*These items transfer to your Balance Sheet (Activity 31).
All other items transfer to your Profit and Loss Statement (Activity 29).

quarterly totals, every quarter total each category for that quarter and transfer to the Profit and Loss Statement (Activity 29) and the Balance Sheet (Activity 31).

c. Some items on your Disbursements Summary, such as furniture and equipment, will transfer to Assets on the Balance Sheet. Most items (advertising, auto expenses, etc.) will transfer to Expenses on the Profit and Loss Statement. On the Disbursements Summary Sample, items marked with an asterisk (*) transfer to Assets, Liabilities, Net Worth, and (Income) Refunds.

d. A note on automobile expenses: If you use your car for both business and personal trips, you can deduct only the business portion for tax purposes. Record odometer readings at the beginning and end of each year to know the total number of miles you have driven, and maintain a record of all your business mileage. Use either a mileage book or your appointment book. At the end of the year your accountant can determine if it is better for you to take the standard mileage deduction or calculate the percentage of actual expenses.

e. Be sure to keep travel expenses separate from entertainment expenses. Recent changes in tax law allow only 80 percent of entertainment costs to be deducted. Give your accountant the total you spent for entertainment, and he or she will calculate the appropriate amount for your Schedule C.

10. **Petty Cash.** If you often make small cash purchases, you will need a Petty Cash Account. See Activity 33 to set one up.

11. **Bank Reconciliation.** It is important to balance your bank account monthly, especially if you have many deposits and checks, if you tend to maintain a low balance, or if you periodically overdraw your account. By regularly performing this simple task, you will know that the balance in your checkbook register is correct. Knowing how much money you have enables you to make solid decisions. When you are careful with your account, reconciling your statement should take only fifteen to twenty minutes per month. If you don't want to do it, pay someone else to do it. If you don't know how, see Activity 34 for instructions.

12. **So, how did it go?**
    a. Describe the fears, resistances, or self-limiting patterns you experienced while completing this activity. What will you do about them?

    b. How were your financial management skills and confidence enhanced?

    c. Reflect on the important points in this activity and describe the clarity you have gained.

    d. What must you learn and develop? What resources will you draw on to build strength? What steps will you take to fulfill these?

◆

Section 3. Financial Matters

Financial Statements

The major objectives of a business are stability, profitability, and solvency. As your business adequately fulfills your needs, makes a steady profit, and pays all your debts when they are due, your stability and inner calm will allow you to add new goals. The financial statements that reflect these conditions are the Profit and Loss Statement (Activity 29), the Variance Statement (Activity 30), and the Balance Sheet (Activity 31).

Normally, when presenting the accounting process, the Balance Sheet is discussed first. However, we feel that its complexity reduces its usefulness for most individuals in a service business, so we present it later. We begin with the Profit and Loss Statement, which is necessary to compute tax payments and determine your net income.

The Profit and Loss Statement

The Profit and Loss Statement reports your profits, which are determined by deducting your expenses from your income. If income exceeds expenses, you are making a profit. If not, you are creating a loss, and to create profit and stability, change is needed. The Profit and Loss Statement also provides financial data from which you can project income, prepare budgets, and calculate taxes.

Activity 29. Profit & Loss Statement

Note: The Profit and Loss Statement reveals net income or net loss—the difference between income and expenses. This figure is transferred to the Balance Sheet (Activity 31) so that your net income or net loss may be added to or deducted from the net worth of your business. Income is transferred from your Receipts Summary. Expenses are transferred from your Disbursements Summary.

1. Make a copy of the Profit and Loss Statement Worksheet on Pages 148 and 149 and study Sample Profit and Loss Statement on Page 147.

2. If you do not have an accountant providing you with monthly Profit and Loss Statements, you may choose to prepare one monthly, quarterly, semiannually, or annually for tax computation. Begin by writing on your worksheet your business name and the beginning and ending dates for this Profit and Loss Statement.

3. For a monthly report, transfer onto the worksheet the figures from your Receipts and Disbursements Summaries for the month indicated. For a quarterly or semiannual report, add together the totals from the Receipts and Disbursements Summaries for the period indicated, and transfer to the worksheet.

    Note: Some entries in your Receipts and Disbursements Journals will transfer to the Balance Sheet (Activity 31), rather than to this worksheet. Therefore, you will need to recalculate Total Income and Total Expenses figures from your summaries for this Profit and Loss Statement, when these are present. Review Activity 25, Chart of Accounts, for assistance.

4. List your income-generating programs, beginning with most and ending with least. Enter amounts from your Receipts Summary (Activity 27, Question 10). Total.

5. List expenses in alphabetical order. Enter figures from your Disbursements Summary (Activity 28, Question 9), except where noted, then total. The more specific the detail, the easier future budgeting and projections will be.

6. Subtract Total Expenses from Total Income. If the difference is positive, enter on the Net Profit line. If negative, enter on the Net Loss line, in brackets. Transfer this number to your Balance Sheet (Activity 31).

7. If desired, calculate the Percentage of Income for each entry, using the following formula
    Income or Expense ÷ Total Income x 100 = % of Income.
    Round off to whole numbers (i.e., enter 10, not 9.8). Because of the rounding, the percent total usually will not equal exactly 100.

    By expressing each figure as a percentage of total income, you can compare program income to total income and specific expenses to total income to decide if your energies and resources are being expended appropriately. For example, the Sample Profit and Loss Statement shows that Mr. Johnson earns only 9 percent of his income from workshops. His copying and printing expenses, most of which relate to workshops, represent 17 percent of his income. After comparing these figures, Mr. Johnson may decide to make some changes with workshops.

8. **So, how did it go?**

    a. Recall and describe the fears, resistances, or self-limiting patterns you experienced while completing this activity. List them in order of priority and explain what you are ready to do about them.

    b. What fears or resistances were you able to release? Explain.

    c. What have you realized that you already knew about Profit and Loss Statements?

    d. What must you learn and develop? What resources are you ready to draw on? List the steps you will take and include dates, when appropriate.

◆

Section 3. Financial Matters

Sample Profit and Loss Statement

```
                ROBERT R. JOHNSON
              PROFIT AND LOSS STATEMENT
           January 1, 1991 to March 31, 1991
```

INCOME	Amount	% of Total Income
Family Counseling	$5,735.00	61
Individual Counseling	2,820.00	30
Workshops	855.00	9
Refunds	<40.00>	—
Interest Income	22.31	—
Service Charges	10.00	—
Miscellaneous Income		
Total Income	**$9,402.31**	**100%**
EXPENSES		
Accounting and Legal	150.00	2
Advertising	369.91	4
Automobile Expenses	1,039.27	11
Bank Charges	10.15	—
Business or Trade Seminars	90.00	1
Contract Services	433.00	5
Copying and Printing	1,587.02	17
Depreciation	635.75	7
Discounts	80.00	1
Dues, Subscriptions, Memberships	90.00	1
Entertainment	444.50	5
Equipment Leasing/Rental	162.00	2
Interest	65.18	1
Miscellaneous	5.99	—
Office Supplies	121.47	1
Postage	105.00	1
Promotion	250.00	2
Rent	855.00	9
Telephone	206.22	2
Utilities	78.40	1
Total Expenses	**$6,778.86**	**72**
NET PROFIT	**$2,623.45**	**28**

Profit and Loss Statement Worksheet

Make copies of this form and use it as an original.

Your Business Name: _____

Profit and Loss Statement
Beginning and Ending Dates: _____ to _____
(ending date same as date on Balance Sheet)

INCOME	Amount	% of Income
Program One* (*Replace these words with your Program Title)		
Program Two*	_____	_____
Program Three*	_____	_____
Refunds (from Disbursements Summary - bracket this amount)	_____	_____
Interest Income	_____	_____
Service Charges	_____	_____
Miscellaneous Income	_____	_____
_____	_____	_____
_____	_____	_____
_____	_____	_____
Total Income	_____	_____
	_____	_____

EXPENSES	Amount	% of Income
Accounting and Legal		
Advertising	_____	_____
Automobile Expenses	_____	_____
Bank Charges	_____	_____
Business or Trade Seminars	_____	_____
Contract Services	_____	_____
Copying	_____	_____
Depreciation (from accountant)	_____	_____
Discounts (from Discount Schedule)	_____	_____
	_____	_____

	Amount	% of Income
Dues, Subscriptions, Memberships		
Entertainment		
Equipment Leasing and Rental		
Fees and Licenses		
Insurance		
Interest Expense		
Laundry		
Miscellaneous		
Office Supplies		
Other Supplies		
Postage		
Promotion		
Promotional Materials		
Rent		
Repairs and Maintenance		
Sales Commissions		
Telephone		
Travel		
Utilities		
_____		
_____		
_____		
Total Expenses		
NET PROFIT		
NET LOSS *(bracket this figure)*		

Note: This Profit and Loss Statement is for both tax filing purposes and your management use. Your accountant or tax consultant will consolidate your income and expenses from this worksheet to prepare Schedule C to file with your income tax return.

Empowering Vision

Variance Statement

A Variance Statement is the financial tool for comparing your budget projections (Activity 26) with your actual income and expenses as reflected on your Profit and Loss Statement (Activity 29).

The Variance Statement shows how accurate you were with your projections, and where your predictions were incorrect. From these figures, you can review your budgeting notes to recall how you determined a projection and to remember the circumstances under which the actual transaction occurred. You can then determine whether an unusual event occurred or if your predictions were simply off and budget adjustments are needed.

For example, if a $50 variance occurred because your rent was raised, your budget should be changed. On the other hand, if 2,000 brochures were ruined by a leak in the roof and had to be reprinted, this is an unusual occurrence you could not have predicted. As you study the variances between budgeted and actual amounts, you will sharpen your management skills. With experience, your projections will become more accurate.

A Variance Statement is most useful if it is prepared monthly. If you budgeted for a quarter, divide your Budget amounts by three to obtain average figures for each month. Where averaging is not appropriate, look at your budgeting notes to determine definite amounts for a specific period.

Activity 30. Variance Statement

Note: Refer to the Variance Worksheet, Page 153, and Variance Statement Sample, Page 152, as you follow these instructions.

1. Study the Variance Statement Sample and enter the month or quarter on a copy of the Variance Statement Worksheet.

2. Fill in the Budget column on your Variance Statement Worksheet using the figures from your Budget, including the totals.

3. Fill in the Actual column on the worksheet using the figures from your Profit and Loss Statement or Cash Receipts and Disbursements Summaries, including the totals.

4. Calculate the Variance column by subtracting the Budget figures from the Actual figures. Bracket negative figures: <253.27>.

    a. For Income, positive numbers indicate your income was more than you budgeted; negative <bracketed> figures indicate your income was less than you budgeted.

b. For Expenses, positive numbers indicate you spent more than you budgeted. Negative <bracketed> figures indicate you spent less than you budgeted.

5. To obtain Total Income Variance, add the figures in the Variance column. Be sure to subtract all bracketed figures. Bracket the total if it is a negative number. Check your math by subtracting Total Budget from Total Actual. The difference should be the same as your Total Variance. If not, you have made an error and need to review your figures. Repeat this process to obtain the Total Expenses Variance.

6. Determine Total Variance by subtracting Total Expenses Variance from Total Income Variance for each of the three columns. If any figure is negative, bracket it—this indicates a loss. Check your math by subtracting the Total Budget from the Total Actual. The result should be the same as the Total Variance.

7. Analyze the Variance Statement by carefully evaluating the circumstances that caused each large variance. Study the notes on the Variance Statement Sample. Add notes to your own statement to explain your variances so you can remember the circumstances when you prepare your next budget. Consider the following:

    a. For Income Variances: Negative numbers indicate that you overprojected, underpromoted or undercharged, offered the program at a low point in your income cycle, or offered a program people weren't ready to buy. Positive numbers indicate you either received unexpected income or received more than anticipated.

    b. For Expense Variances: Negative numbers indicate you spent less than you budgeted. You may have been liberal in your expense projections, you may have forgotten to include an expense from your Profit & Loss Statement, or something you thought would result in an expense did not occur. Positive numbers may indicate you were conservative in your expense projections, forgot to project an expense, or experienced an unexpected event.

    c. Total Variance: The Total Variance figure allows you to compare your Total Actual expenses with Actual Income and your Total Budget with Income. A positive variance total means that when you prepared your budget you underestimated your income and/or overestimated your expenses. If your Total Variance was negative, you may have been too optimistic, with income, experienced unforeseen expenses, or made made expenditures without consulting your budget. As your financial skills develop, your variances will begin to approach zero, barring unforeseen circumstances.

8. What fears or resistances were you able to release? Explain.

9. What must you learn and develop? List the steps you will take and include dates, when appropriate.

◆

Empowering Vision

Sample Variance Statement

ROBERT R. JOHNSON
VARIANCE SUMMARY
January, 1991

	BUDGET	ACTUAL	VARIANCE
INCOME			
Family Counseling	$ 925.00	1,850.00	925.00[1]
Individual Counseling	640.00	900.00	260.00[2]
Workshops	285.00	285.00	0.00
Interest	10.00	6.85	<3.15>
Service Charge	10.00	10.00	0.00
Total Income Variance	$1,870.00	3,051.85	1,181.85
EXPENSES			
Advertising	$ 0.00	123.22	123.22[3]
Automobile Expenses	250.00	467.30	217.30[4]
Business Seminars	30.00	90.00	60.00[5]
Contract Services	100.00	108.00	8.00
Copying and Printing	100.00	23.02	<76.98>[5]
Dues/Subscriptions	50.00	90.00	40.00[5]
Entertainment	50.00	133.09	83.09[7]
Equipment Rental	100.00	54.00	<46.00>[6]
Note	200.00	166.47	<33.53>
Office Supplies/Postage	75.00	67.68	<7.32>
Rent	285.00	285.00	0.00
Telephone	75.00	68.74	<6.26>
Utilities	100.00	0.00	<100.00>[8]
Miscellaneous	200.00	28.60	<171.40>[9]
Total Expenses Variance	$1,615.00	1,705.12	90.12
TOTAL VARIANCE	255.00	1,346.73	1,091.73

Notes:
1. Budgeted for 5 clients; got 10.
2. Budgeted for 4 clients; got 6.
3. Forgot to include in budget. Add.
4. Fuel pump broke.
5. Budgeted for the year, then divided by 12 to get monthly amount. Over the year, should average out to budget figure.
6. Equipment Rental less than anticipated. Adjust Budget.
7. Higher than anticipated. Adjust Budget if expenses continue to be high.
8. Utilities billed every three months.
9. Bank charges, interest, miscellaneous; unsure about actual costs.

Variance Statement Worksheet

Make copies of this form and use it as an original.

VARIANCE SUMMARY

Month/Quarter: _____ 19 __

	BUDGET	ACTUAL	VARIANCE
INCOME			
Program One* (*Replace these words with your Program Title)	_____	_____	_____
Program Two*	_____	_____	_____
Program Three*	_____	_____	_____
Refunds	_____	_____	_____
Interest	_____	_____	_____
Miscellaneous	_____	_____	_____
Service Charges	_____	_____	_____
_____	_____	_____	_____
_____	_____	_____	_____
_____	_____	_____	_____
Total Income	═══════	═══════	═══════
EXPENSES			
Accounting and Legal	_____	_____	_____
Advertising	_____	_____	_____
Automobile Expenses	_____	_____	_____
Bank Charges	_____	_____	_____
Business/Trade Seminars	_____	_____	_____
Contract Services	_____	_____	_____
Copying	_____	_____	_____
Discounts	_____	_____	_____
Dues/Subscriptions	_____	_____	_____
Entertainment	_____	_____	_____
Equipment Rental	_____	_____	_____

	BUDGET	ACTUAL	VARIANCE
Fees and Licenses	_____	_____	_____
Insurance	_____	_____	_____
Interest	_____	_____	_____
Laundry	_____	_____	_____
Note	_____	_____	_____
Office Supplies	_____	_____	_____
Other Supplies	_____	_____	_____
Postage	_____	_____	_____
Promotion	_____	_____	_____
Promotional Materials	_____	_____	_____
Rent	_____	_____	_____
Repairs/Maintenance	_____	_____	_____
Sales Commissions	_____	_____	_____
Telephone	_____	_____	_____
Travel	_____	_____	_____
Utilities	_____	_____	_____
Miscellaneous	_____	_____	_____
_____	_____	_____	_____
_____	_____	_____	_____
_____	_____	_____	_____
Total Expenses	_____	_____	_____
TOTAL VARIANCE	_____	_____	_____

Section 3. Financial Matters

The Balance Sheet

A Balance Sheet reveals the financial condition of your business at a given point in time. It shows the mix and strength of your assets, your total liabilities, and your equity (or net worth).

- **Assets** are the things of value that you need to offer your service: cash, furniture and fixtures, equipment, anything owned by your business.

- **Liabilities** are your business debts—short-term loans and long-term notes—due at specific times.

- **Net Worth** is the personal money, equipment, and other assets that you have invested in your business, minus draws for your personal income, and plus or minus your business profits or losses up to the statement date. It is derived by subtracting your liabilities from your assets.

The Balance Sheet shows, as of a specific date, the value of and relationship between your business assets, debts, and net worth. The Balance Sheet is based on this accounting equation:
Assets = Liabilities + Net Worth.

*"You are prosperous
to the degree that you are experiencing
peace, health, and plenty in your world."*
Catherine Ponder

Activity 31. Balance Sheet

*Note: Make copies of this worksheet to use as an original.
Not all of the accounts listed will apply to your business.*

BALANCE SHEET

Your Company Name: _____

Ending Date (same as P&L): _____

1. **ASSETS:** These range in descending order from the most liquid, or accessible, to the least (i.e., from your checking account to leasehold improvements). Begin with your checking, savings, and money market balances as of the Balance Sheet date you select. Next, carry forward any amounts unchanged from previous Balance Sheets (such as equipment) and add new assets as recorded in your Disbursements Summary (Activity 28, Question 9), except where other instructions are provided.

Empowering Vision

If you have sold any assets, ask your accountant how to adjust your Balance Sheet. As of your Balance Sheet date, complete the following:

Cash in Bank - Checking (balance in checkbook
   (register on Balance Sheet date)   _____

Cash in Bank - Savings   _____

Money Market Account   _____

Petty Cash (initial amounts, not replenishment)   _____

Equipment   _____

Furniture and Fixtures   _____

Leasehold Improvements   _____

Other   _____

Total Assets   _____

2. **LIABILITIES:** As of your Balance Sheet date, using figures from your Disbursements Summary (Activity 28, Question 9), add any new short-term loans and notes. Complete the following:

Short-Term Loans (amount from last Balance Sheet reduced
   or increased by amounts paid since last Balance Sheet.
   List individually on a separate sheet)   _____

Notes (amount from last Balance Sheet reduced or increased
   by amounts paid since last Balance Sheet. List
   individually on a separate sheet)   _____

Total Liabilities   _____

3. **NET WORTH:** Complete Activity 29, Profit and Loss Statement. To calculate Net Worth, subtract Total Liabilities from Total Assets and fill in on Total Net Worth line below. Fill in all lines below except Equity. Calculate equity: Net Worth + Draw - Net Profit = Equity. Fill in on Equity line.

Equity   _____

Draw (bracket this amount)   _____

   Current Year's Net Profit (from Profit and Loss Statement)   _____

   Current Year's Net Loss (from Profit and Loss Statement.
      Bracket this amount.)   _____

Total Net Worth   _____

Add Total Liablilites, plus Net Worth and fill in. This figure should be the same as your Total Assets. Total Assets, less Total Liabilites, should equal Total Net Worth.   _____

TOTAL LIABILITIES AND NET WORTH   _____

Sample Balance Sheet

```
         ROBERT R. JOHNSON
           BALANCE SHEET
           March 31, 1991
```

ASSETS

Cash in Bank - Checking	$1,206.90
Cash in Bank - Savings	200.00
Money Market Account	100.00
Petty Cash	50.00
Equipment	2,543.19
Total Assets	**$4,100.09**

LIABILITIES

Short-Term Loans	
Notes	997.70*
Total Liabilities	**$ 997.70**

NET WORTH

Equity	$2,578.94
Draw	<2,100.00>
Net Profit, 3/31/91	2,623.45
Total Net Worth	**$3,102.39**

TOTAL LIABILITIES & NET WORTH   **$4,100.09**

* Mr. Johnson has a note for $1,500. He paid $502.30 on the principal (see Disbursements Summary, line 19), so as of March 31, he owes $997.70.

Empowering Vision

So, how did it go?

1. Describe the fears, resistances, or self-limiting patterns you experienced while completing this activity. What will you do about them?

2. Describe how your financial management skills have been enhanced.

3. Describe how you feel more confident.

4. Reflect on the important points in this activity and describe the clarity you have gained.

5. What have you discovered that you already knew about a balance sheet?

6. What have you determined that you need to learn about a balance sheet? What resources are you ready to draw on? List the steps you will take and include dates, when appropriate.

◆

negotiate sales — *yes* — *vision* — *agreements* — *goals* — *timelines* — *financial integrity* — *ease* — *quality* — *caring* — *prosperity* — *honesty* — *security* — *income* — *comfort* — *investment* — *stability* — *savings* — *confidence* — *skill* — *abundance* — *assets* — *fees* — *taxes* — *appreciation* — *success* — *well-being*

"... there is only one way by which you can achieve prosperity. It is to take charge of your mind."
Eric Butterworth

158

Section 3. Financial Matters

Taxes

It would be impossible to include a comprehensive tax guide in this manual because of the complexity of the tax laws and the frequency with which they change. However, a brief explanation of the requirements you face regarding income tax and social security payments is in order. Check with your accountant, attorney, and/or your state's Department of Revenue regarding tax payments for which you may be liable.

As a sole proprietor, you must file Schedule C, *Profit (or Loss) From Business or Profession*, and Schedule SE, *Computation of Social Security Self-Employment Tax*, with your federal income tax return. (If your business is a partnership or a corporation, refer to the section on Basic Organizational Structures (Pages 119 and 120) and see your accountant about filing requirements.) The mandatory self-employment tax allows you to be eligible for social security benefits, just as wage earners are. The 1990 social security tax for the self-employed is 12.4 percent for the first $53,400 earned, and 2.9 percent for the medicare tax for the first $125,00 earned, totalling 15.3 percent. However, changes in the tax law allow for a deduction of 1/2 this self-employment tax as an adjustment to gross income. See your accountant for the correct handling of your taxes.

Because you do not have an employer to withhold income and social security taxes from your earnings, you must file Form 1040-ES, *Tax Withholding and Estimated Tax*, which covers payments for both income and social security taxes. Check with your state's Department of Revenue for their requirements regarding income, self-employment, and estimated taxes. To calculate your quarterly tax payments, consider the following: If your income is stable or increasing from year to year, divide last year's tax liability by four and pay that amount each time your tax payment is due (April 15, July 15, September 15, and January 15). This method takes the least amount of time and eliminates any penalties. However, if your income has increased, be sure to save approximately 20 percent of your net profit to cover the taxes that will be due when you file your personal return. If your income will be less than last year's, there are other ways to compute the amount you owe. Discuss these with your accountant.

Note: It is easier and more cost effective to keep up with these calculations each quarter than it is to put them off until your annual filing. The IRS assesses penalties and interest for late payments, which are probably far greater than the fee you will pay to have your taxes prepared by an accountant, and the peace of mind is well worth it. For more information, obtain the following IRS publications: 334, *Tax Guide for Small Business*; 505, *Tax Withholding and Estimated Tax*; 533, *Self-Employment Tax*; 535, *Business Expenses*; 587, *Business Use of Your Home*; 541, *Tax Information on Partnerships*; 542, *Tax Information on Corporations*; 589, *Tax Information on S Corporations*.

> *"Man should be ready to use past knowledge and skill to meet the demands of a stage yet to come."*
> Dane Rudhyar

Empowering Vision

Sample Schedule C

SCHEDULE C (Form 1040)
Department of the Treasury
Internal Revenue Service (O)

Profit or Loss From Business
(Sole Proprietorship)
Partnerships, Joint Ventures, Etc., Must File Form 1065.
▶ Attach to Form 1040 or Form 1041.   ▶ See Instructions for Schedule C (Form 1040).

OMB No. 1545-0074
1990
Attachment Sequence No. 09

Name of proprietor: Robert R. Johnson
Social security number (SSN): 123:45:6789

A Principal business or profession, including product or service (see Instructions): Psychologist
B Enter principal business code (from page 2) ▶ 8|7|5|5|

C Business name and address (include suite or room no.) ▶ 135 Main Street, Anytown, CO 80999
D Employer ID number (Not SSN):

E Accounting method: (1) ☒ Cash   (2) ☐ Accrual   (3) ☐ Other (specify) ▶

F Method(s) used to value closing inventory: (1) ☐ Cost   (2) ☐ Lower of cost or market   (3) ☐ Other (attach explanation)   (4) ☐ Does not apply (if checked, go to line H)

		Yes	No
G	Was there any change in determining quantities, costs, or valuations between opening and closing inventory? (If "Yes," attach explanation.)		X
H	Are you deducting expenses for business use of your home? (If "Yes," see Instructions for limitations.)		X
I	Did you "materially participate" in the operation of this business during 1990? (If "No," see Instructions for limitations on losses.)		
J	If this is the first Schedule C filed for this business, check here ▶ ☐		

Part I Income

1	Gross receipts or sales. **Caution:** If this income was reported to you on Form W-2 and the "Statutory employee" box on that form was checked, see the Instructions and check here ▶ ☐	1	46,315 —
2	Returns and allowances	2	
3	Subtract line 2 from line 1. Enter the result here	3	46,315 —
4	Cost of goods sold (from line 38 on page 2)	4	
5	Subtract line 4 from line 3 and enter the **gross profit** here	5	46,315 —
6	Other income, including Federal and state gasoline or fuel tax credit or refund (see Instructions)	6	181 45
7	Add lines 5 and 6. This is your **gross income** ▶	7	46,496 45

Part II Expenses

8	Advertising	8	5,375 53	21 Repairs and maintenance	21	
9	Bad debts from sales or services (see Instructions)	9		22 Supplies (not included in Part III)	22	528 81
10	Car and truck expenses (attach Form 4562)	10	2,096 34	23 Taxes and licenses	23	1,000 —
11	Commissions and fees	11	11 —	24 Travel, meals, and entertainment:		
12	Depletion	12		**a** Travel	24a	
13	Depreciation and section 179 expense deduction (not included in Part III) (see Instructions)	13	1,175 —	**b** Meals and entertainment		446 48
				c Enter 20% of line 24b subject to limitations (see Instructions)		
14	Employee benefit programs (other than on line 19)	14		**d** Subtract line 24c from line 24b	24d	446 48
15	Insurance (other than health)	15		25 Utilities	25	1,178 16
16	Interest:			26 Wages (less jobs credit)	26	
	a Mortgage (paid to banks, etc.)	16a		27a Other expenses (list type and amount):		
	b Other	16b	220 17	Contract Services 1,916 —		
17	Legal and professional services	17	1,050 —	Prof. Education 270 —		
18	Office expense	18	2,343 53			
19	Pension and profit-sharing plans	19				
20	Rent or lease (see Instructions):					
	a Vehicles, machinery, and equip.	20a	324 —			
	b Other business property	20b	3,420 —	27b Total other expenses	27b	2,186 —
28	Add amounts in columns for lines 8 through 27b. These are your **total expenses** ▶				28	21,355 02
29	Net profit or (loss). Subtract line 28 from line 7. If a profit, enter here and on Form 1040, line 12. Also enter the net profit on Schedule SE, line 2 (statutory employees, see Instructions). If a loss, you MUST go on to line 30 (fiduciaries, see Instructions)				29	25,141 43

30 If you have a loss, you MUST check the box that describes your investment in this activity (see Instructions).
  30a ☐ All investment is at risk.
  30b ☐ Some investment is not at risk.

If you checked 30a, enter the loss on Form 1040, line 12, and Schedule SE, line 2 (statutory employees, see Instructions). If you checked 30b, you MUST attach **Form 6198**.

For Paperwork Reduction Act Notice, see Form 1040 Instructions.   Schedule C (Form 1040) 1990

Your Break-even Point

Calculating the break-even point allows you to determine the financial viability of a new or current program and your business as a whole. At the break-even point, your income and expenses are equal. Above this point, therefore, income exceeds expenses and you create a profit; below this point, expenses exceed income and you experience a loss.

Calculating break-even is accomplished by translating your program's expenses into the simple formula described in Activity 32. With this figure, you can determine if your fees and the number of clients you project are adequate and whether your program is viable, based on the cash flow it will produce. Remember that your personal income is created from your profit.

Fixed and Variable Expenses

To calculate your break-even point, assign each of your expenses to either the fixed or variable category.

Fixed expenses are the necessary costs you must pay in order to be in business and to offer your program. Fixed expenses recur regularly, perhaps each time you offer your program, whether it is intermittent or ongoing. Fixed expenses do not depend on how much business or how many clients you have. Examples of fixed expenses include:

Fixed Overhead Expenses	Fixed Program Expenses
office rent	workshop space rental
base monthly telephone rate	promotional materials
lease payments for furniture or equipment	advertising
office supplies	postage

Variable expenses depend on the number of clients you serve and on the unique requirements of your income-generating program, marketing strategy, and operating costs. Variable expenses, therefore, directly relate to both the type of service you offer and your workload. Examples of variable expenses include:

Variable Overhead Expenses	Variable Program Expenses
copying	workshop handouts
entertainment	workshop refreshments
long distance charges	chair rental

Empowering Vision

✍ Activity 32. Break-even Calculation

1. **Determine Time Period.** Determine the time period you want the income from this program to cover.

2. **Determine Fee.** State the fee per client for your program. For guidelines on determining your fees, see Activity 11, Question 10, and Activity 13, Question 1. (The fee for our sample workshop is $100 per client.)

3. **Determine Overhead Expenses.** Categorize, as fixed, all your monthly business overhead expenses from your budget or Activity 5, Organizing Your Business, Question 9. In addition, determine the amount and percentage of overhead expense you want this program to generate in the time period you choose. (You calculated these program percentages in Activity 12, Question 8.) For example:

   - If you have only one program, include 100 percent of your overhead expenses in the break-even calculation.

   - If you have several programs, each of which contributes equally to your total income, then, depending on the number of programs, allocate the appropriate percentage (50 percent, 33 percent, 25 percent, etc.) of your overhead expense to each program.

   - If you have several programs that contribute varying amounts to your total income (say 50 percent, 30 percent, and 20 percent), include the appropriate percentage of total overhead expense in your break-even calculation.

   - If you want only to figure the breakeven point for the program, do not include business overhead. Include only the program expenses you will list in Question 4.

4. **Determine Program Expenses.** Categorize the program expenses from your budget or those you listed in Program Planning and Development, Activity 11, Question 11, into both Fixed and Variable. If you are unsure whether an expense is fixed or variable, ask your mentor for help, or include it in the fixed category. Review the following sample list of expenses for a workshop:

FIXED		VARIABLE	
(Expenses per session regardless of number of clients)		*(Expenses per client)*	
Workshop space rental	$ 50	Handouts	$10
Promotional materials	100	Refreshments	2
Advertising	500	Chair Rental	1
Postage	50		
Overhead (1/3 of 1,500)	500		
Total Fixed Expenses	$1,200	Total Variable Expenses	$13

Section 3. Financial Matters

5. **Calculate the Break-even Point.** Use the following formula to determine your program's break-even point. (Directions for using the formula are included in a-d below.)

$$\frac{\text{Total Fixed Expenses}}{1 - \dfrac{\text{Variable Expenses per Client}}{\text{Fee per Client}}} = \text{Program Income Break-even Point}$$

Using the numbers in our sample, our break-even point is:

$$\frac{\$1{,}200}{1 - 13/100} = \frac{\$1{,}200}{1 - .13} = \frac{\$1{,}200}{.87} = \frac{\$1{,}379.31}{100} = 13.8 \text{ clients, or } 14 \text{ clients @ \$100 each}$$

Note: To calculate the break-even point using this formula, follow these steps:

a. Divide Variable Expenses per Client by Fee per Client (in our sample, 13 divided by 100 = .13). This number, .13, representing the relationship between expenses and fees, is called a ratio.

b. Subtract this ratio from 1 (1 - .13 = .87).

c. Divide this amount into Total Fixed Expenses (1,200 ÷ by .87 = 1,379). Your answer will show you how much you need to earn from that session or your program in order to break even. Note that break-even covers your business expenses, not your personal income, which comes from profit (see Question 5 below).

d. Divide the program income break-even point, your answer from c, (1379) by your fee per client (100). This answer indicates the number of clients required to break even. (In our sample, the result is 13.8 clients, rounded up to 14.)

6. **Calculate Profit.** Profit includes your personal income and additional money you can reinvest in your business. To calculate profit, use the formula:

$$\text{Profit} = \text{Income} - \text{Expenses}$$

To calculate our profit from 14 clients at $100 per client, remembering that our fixed expenses are $1,200 and variable expenses are $13 per client:

Profit = 14×$100 - ($1,200 + 14×$13) = $1,400 - ($1,200 + $182) = $1,400 - $1,382 = $18

$18 is not enough to provide for your personal income. If we choose to limit the number of clients in the workshop, we could raise the fee to show more profit. If we want a maximum of 12 clients, for example, we could set the fee at $175 to make this profit:

Profit = (12×$175) - $1,200 + (12×$13) = $2,100 - ($1,200 + $156) = $2,100 - $1,356 = $744

Or, we could increase the number of clients, with or without a fee increase:

Empowering Vision

Profit = (18x$175) - $1,200 + (18x$13) = $3,150 - ($1,200 + $234) = $3,150 - $1,434 = $1,716

Note: Determine how you can make a reasonable profit with the income and expense projections you used. If the profit is not adequate, you can raise your fees, lower your expenses, or both. Or, you can increase the number of clients required for the program. For each scenario, recalculate your break-even until you are satisfied.

This graph shows our sample in a different format for our sample break-even in Question 5.

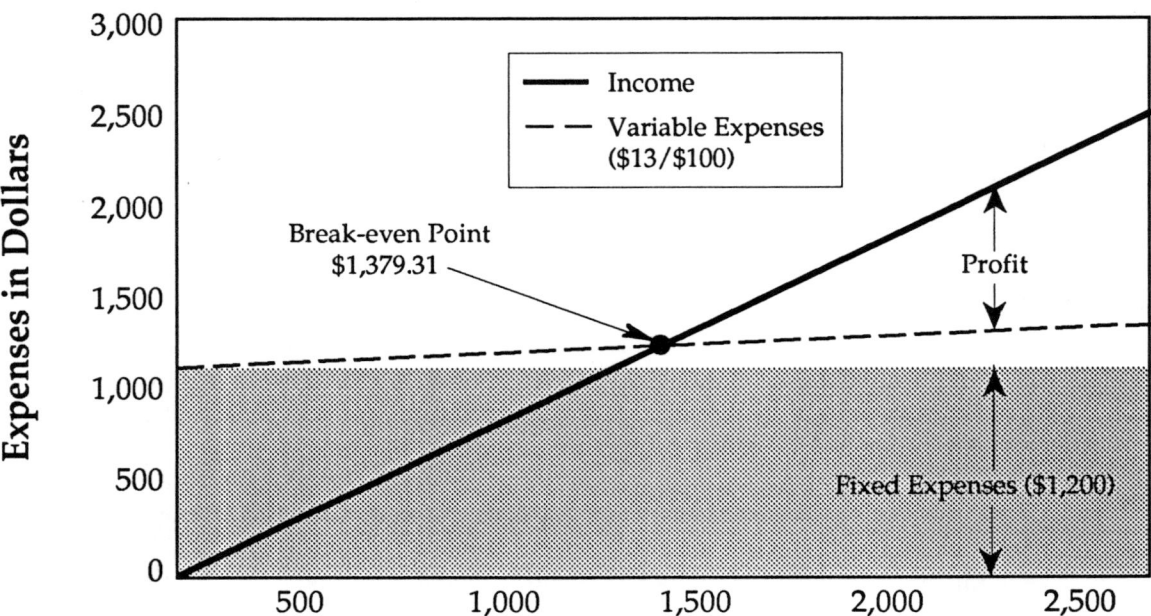

7. **So, how did it go?**

   a. Recall and describe the fears, resistances, or self-limiting patterns you experienced while completing this activity. List them in order of priority and explain what you are ready to do about them.

   b. What fears or resistances were you able to release? Explain.

   c. Reflect on the important points this activity revealed to you and describe how you feel empowered.

   d. What must you learn and develop as a business manager? What resources are you ready to draw on? How can your mentors help you? List the steps you will take and include dates, when appropriate.

◆

Section 3. Financial Matters

Petty Cash Account

Most self-employed people pay for some of their business expenses with personal money: copying, gasoline, supplies, postage, and so forth. Unless a system is created to keep track of these small amounts, they won't be included with expenses from the Cash Disbursements Journal, and help reduce the tax liability.

A petty cash account is used for these cash purchases for your business. It is easiest to set up a separate container or envelope from which you make cash purchases and into which you put receipts and your Petty Cash Record. (You may use the form on Page 167). Review the Sample Petty Cash Record on Page 166.

Activity 33. Petty Cash

1. Write a check payable to Cash for $50, $75, or $100, depending on how frequently you intend to make cash purchases. ($50 is used in our sample.) Record this check in the Miscellaneous column of your Disbursements Journal as Petty Cash..

2. Cash the check and put the money in an envelope or container, along with a copy of the Petty Cash Record on Page 167. In the first row on your record, enter the date and write $50 under Balance on Hand. (See Sample on Page 166.)

3. As you use this money, always enclose the receipt and fill out the next line on the Record.

4. When the balance on hand drops to about $10, create a Summary on the Petty Cash Record, adding together like expenses. (See Sample Summary on Page 166.)

5. Add your expenses and deduct from $50, which should equal the remaining cash. If not, recalculate to determine the accurate figures. If your remaining cash does not equal the expenses deducted from the initial $50, write the difference as "Misc." and include it in the Summary. Write "unlocated error" next to Misc. If you have more money than your receipts account for, you will bracket < > the amount.

6. Write another check, payable to Cash for $50 minus your balance on hand, to replenish your Petty Cash. (In our sample, the check is for $47.55.)

7. Begin a new Petty Cash Record with your new balance on hand of $50.

8. In your Disbursements Journal, enter the amounts from the Petty Cash Summary in the appropriate expense columns. (See line 24 on Sample Disbursements Journal.) Staple the cash receipts to the Petty Cash Record and file it in your business receipts file under Petty Cash.

◆

Sample Petty Cash Record

\	PETTY CASH RECORD			
Date	Paid To	For	Amount	Balance
1/3				50.00
1/5	ABC Office Supply	Office Supplies	5.10	44.90
1/10	Eads	Education	3.20	41.70
1/11	Lucille's	Entertainment	8.50	33.20
1/15	Postmaster	Postage	11.00	22.20
1/21	ABC Office Supply	Supplies	5.75	16.45
1/25	Postmaster	Postage	11.00	5.45
1/26	Denny's	Entertainment	3.00	2.45
		Summary		
		Office Supplies		10.85
		Postage		22.00
		Entertainment		11.50
		Education		3.20
		Total		47.55

Make copies of this form and use it as an original.

PETTY CASH RECORD				
Date	Paid To	For	Amount	Balance

© Empowering Vision

Empowering Vision

Reconciling Your Checkbook Balance

Some people don't know how much money they have or the value of the things they own. Nor do they understand the laws that govern the use of these for taxation purposes. Consequently, they don't know how to manage them within the laws of our legal system.

Some people in business for themselves even refuse to learn about effective money management. Although they provide a quality service or product, they experience anxiety, stress, and strain in managing their business.

Sound familiar? If so, and if you are ready to change this pattern into a mindset and foundation conducive to sound decision-making, begin by always balancing your bank statement within a few days of receiving it.

Balancing your bank statement monthly is simple. If you are self-employed in a service business, reconciling your statement will take from 10-20 minutes per month. In the process, your goal is to make sure your checkbook register balance corresponds with the balance on your statement.

✍ Activity 34. Balancing Your Bank Statement

Note: Use the worksheet on Page 170 or the format on the back of your bank statement to balance your account. Follow these instructions:

1. Fill in the ending statement date on Period Ending line.

2. On line 1, fill in the ending balance, as shown on your bank statement.

3. On lines 2-4, add deposits from your checkbook register that are not on the statement as of the statement's ending date.

4. Total after adding deposits (line 5).

5. In the space provided between lines 5 and 6, list all outstanding checks—checks you have written but that haven't cleared your bank and are not listed on the statement. Record the total on line 6.

6. Subtract line 6 from line 5; the figure you obtain is your adjusted bank balance (line 7).

7. Calculate the balance in your checkbook register as of the bank statement's ending date.

8. On line 8, write your checkbook register balance as of the ending date shown on your bank statement.

Section 3. Financial Matters

9. Add any bank credits and interest from the bank statement that you have not entered in your checkbook register, and put the total on line 9.

10. On line 10, put the total of any bank debits and service charges from the statement that you have not yet recorded in your checkbook register.

11. Add lines 8 and 9, then subtract line 10 to obtain your reconciled checkbook balance (line 11).

12. The adjusted bank balance (line 7) should equal the reconciled checkbook balance (line 11). If it does not, make sure you have correctly:

    - Calculated the math on your bank reconciliation
    - Added interest
    - Subtracted all debits, and service charges
    - Entered each check and debit in your checkbook register
    - Entered all bank card and automatic transfer transactions in your register
    - Evaluated the prior month's reconciliation for any details that affect the current reconciliation and brought forward all outstanding checks.
    - Checked all additions and subtractions in your register

13. If you have an error in your bank reconciliation and cannot find it, ask for help from your bank, a friend, or your accountant. If you are not able to correct the error and want to close your books for the month, record it in your Disbursements Journal as an increase or reduction in cash, as appropriate. Record it as "Miscellaneous Expense" in the Miscellaneous column, and highlight it for your accountant. It is best to find the error rather than record an adjustment. Sometimes simple errors can hide major errors.

14. List all bank credits and debits in your checkbook register.

    Note: Remember, mistakes result when you are not concentrating—that is, when you are in a hurry, resisting, or preferring to be doing something else. It takes only a second to make a mistake; finding a mistake takes more time. If you prefer not to do your own bookkeeping, then set up your system the way you want it (especially the Chart of Accounts), and find someone else to keep your books and balance your bank statement for you. The peace of mind, freedom from hassle at tax time, and the small cost will be forever worth it.

15. Reflect on the important points this activity revealed to you and describe the clarity you have gained. How will your financial management and stability be enhanced?

◆

*"Argue for your limitations,
and sure enough, they're yours."*
Richard Bach

Empowering Vision

Sample Bank Reconciliation

Period Ending: _____ January 31, 1991 _____

Enter ending balance from bank statement   1. **235.07**

List deposits made before statement ending date and not on statement   2. **160.00**

3. **185.00**

4. _____

Total of lines 1-4   5. **580.07**

List outstanding checks
(Use this space for additional outstanding checks.)

Ck. #	Amount	Ck. #	Amount
3475	<162.00>		
3477	<48.00>		

Total of outstanding checks   6. **<210.00>**

Adjusted Bank Balance (subtract line 6 from line 5)   7. **370.07**

Enter checkbook register balance on statement ending date   8. **365.93**

Enter total bank credits and interest from statement   9. **6.85**

Enter total debits and service charges from statement   10. **<2.71>**

RECONCILED CHECKBOOK BALANCE (line 8 + line 9 - line 10)   11. **370.07**

Bank Reconciliation Worksheet

Make copies of this form and use it as an original.

Period Ending: _____

Enter ending balance from bank statement   1. _____

List deposits made before statement ending date and not on statement   2. _____

3. _____

4. _____

Total of lines 1-4   5. _____

List outstanding checks
(Use this space for additional outstanding checks.)

Ck. #	Amount	Ck. #	Amount
_____	_____	_____	_____
_____	_____	_____	_____
_____	_____	_____	_____
_____	_____	_____	_____
_____	_____	_____	_____
_____	_____	_____	_____

Total of outstanding checks   6. _____

Adjusted Bank Balance (subtract line 6 from line 5)   7. _____

Enter checkbook register balance on statement ending date   8. _____

Enter total bank credits and interest from statement   9. _____

Enter total debits and service charges from statement   10. _____

RECONCILED CHECKBOOK BALANCE (line 8 + line 9 - line 10)   11. _____

© Empowering Vision

Appendix A.

Glossary

Accounting: a systematic approach to the recording and reporting of business transactions for financial management, taxation, and budgeting purposes.

Accounting Equation: Net Worth = Assets - Liabilities.

Accounts Payable: the amount owed for expenses, not yet paid.

Accounts Receivable: the amount owed by a client, not yet received.

Accrual Basis: an accounting methodology that recognizes revenues when sales are made or services are performed even though cash has not yet been received. Likewise, expenses are recognized as incurred regardless of whether cash has been paid yet. (See also Cash Basis.)

Administration: managing the daily affairs of a business.

Advertising: non-personal, paid-for, media sales presentations.

Agreement: an arrangement between parties outlining the terms of the relationship. (See also Contract and Letter of Agreement.)

Asset: anything with cash value owned by a business.

Balance Sheet: a statement showing the status of the assets, liabilities, and net worth of a business on a specific date.

Bank Charges: amounts deducted from a checking account by the bank for services rendered, as shown on the bank statement.

Bank Credit: amounts added to a checking account, as shown on the bank statement.

Bank Debit: charges deducted from a checking account, as shown on the bank statement.

Bank Reconciliation: an exercise to achieve agreement between the cash balance on the books—the checkbook register—and the bank records—bank statement, making adjustments as necessary.

Bonding: placing a guarantee on an individual to cover losses that result from his or her actions.

Bookkeeping: the act of recording the financial transactions of a business.

Brainstorming: the process of two or more people expressing all the thoughts, ideas, and activities involved in achieving a goal, solving a problem, or making a decision. In brainstorming, there are no judgments or evaluations, but rather a free and spontaneous flow of ideas that stimulate more ideas.

Break-even Analysis: the mathematical or graphical representation of the point at which no profit or loss occurs; used to help make decisions about setting fees, client load, profitability, and discounts for a program.

Budgeting: efficient allocation and projection of resources to realize vision, purpose, and goals.

Business: the profit-making service in which individuals are engaged.

Business Plan: see Business Proposal.

Business Proposal: the written presentation of the business, used for borrowing capital; includes philosophy, description of service, supporting services, marketing strategy, history of business and managers, and financial information, including fees, budgets and financial statements. Also includes future directions and goals.

Calendar Year: year beginning January 1 and ending December 31. (See also Fiscal Year.)

Cash Basis: an accounting system that recognizes revenues when cash is received and recognizes expenses when cash is paid. (See also Accrual Basis.)

Cash on Hand: cash, checks, and bank deposits; listed on the Balance Sheet.

Chart of Accounts: a list of all assets, liabilities, and net worth, as well as income and expense accounts for use with an accounting system.

Client: the one to whom professional services are rendered.

Client Profile: a description of one's target market in demographic and psychographic terms.

Client Service Area: the geographical limitations of the service industry within which one chooses to work.

Cold Call: a direct sales call without prior familiarity or formal introduction.

Collateral: assets that are pledged to secure a loan.

Collections: the process by which overdue payments are collected. Methods of collection include letters, telephone calls, use of a collection agency, lawsuits, and small claims court.

Competition: other people or businesses offering a similar service, theoretically striving to serve the same clientele; can also be those who do not have a similar service but are competing for the same dollar from clients, as seen from the client's point of view.

Complimentary Services: services provided for no charge.

Contract: a written agreement, signed by two or more parties, enforceable by law. (See also Agreement and Letter of Agreement.)

Contract Services: professional services that are obtained and paid on an as-needed basis (rather than employee services or retainer arrangements).

Corporation: a business owned by one person, a few people, or many people; ownership is represented by shares of stock, transferable through their sale or trade.

Cost-Effective: when the benefit and return are greater than the cost/output.

Cover Letter: a brief letter of introduction or explanation of the accompanying information.

CPA (Certified Public Accountant): an accountant who has met state requirements and has been granted a state certificate.

Critical Path Method (CPM) Chart: a time-lined chart used to plan, control, and make decisions about a project in its design and implementation stages.

Current State: present, but not necessarily desired, situation or condition. (See also Preferred State.)

Demographics: general characteristics of a specific population used for making marketing decisions. (See also Psychographics.)

Depreciation: the loss in value of a fixed asset over time, from its original cost to present market value, listed on the Balance Sheet as a reduction in Assets and on the Profit and Loss Statement as an Expense.

Direct Sales: one-to-one sales presentations made by the owner or agent of a business.

Disbursements Journal: the bookkeeping journal in which all cash outflows are recorded, as listed on the Chart of Accounts.

Disbursements Summary: the bookkeeping journal that records monthly and quarterly totals of all expenses from which financial statement figures are recorded.

Discount: a deduction of a specific amount from the usual fee, usually for promotional reasons.

Draw: personal withdrawals from the business account of a sole proprietorship or partnership; not an expense, but a reduction in Owner's Investment, listed on the Balance Sheet.

Dream: the fantasy created within the mind to satisfy unmet needs and desires.

Editor: a person who transforms written drafts into suitable, final copy or documents.

Empower: to enable; to facilitate the emergence of the vital state of aliveness that is generated as we do, well, what we love, want, and are ready to do.

Entrepreneur: an individual who conceives of, organizes, maintains, and assumes the risk of a business venture.

Equity: owner's investment and interest in the business.

Estimated Tax: the tax that must be paid to the IRS and/or state in four installments by individuals having income above a certain level and not subject to withholding.

Evolutionary Need: a transitional individual, societal, or global condition—challenge, conflict, or crisis—that requires a new response, and when resolved, will empower the quality of life.

Evolutionary Purpose: the intention for which a person or thing is directed to effect an evolutionary change.

Expense: a necessary cost of operating a business.

Fair Market Value: net disposable value (current salable value) of an asset.

Financial Management: the act of managing and utilizing money and other assets.

Financial Statements: statements that reflect the profitability (Profit and Loss Statement) and solvency (Balance Sheet) of a business.

Fiscal Year: the accounting of 12 consecutive months, which may or may not coincide with the calendar year. (See also Calendar Year.)

Goals: specific intentions and objectives intended to make one's vision a part of everyday life.

Graphic Artist: a commercial artist who adds artistry—design details and graphic attractiveness, including graphs or illustrations—to the printed materials of a business.

Guarantee: the assumption of responsibility for the quality or proper execution of a product or a service, often written.

Historical Cost: the original cost of an asset; actual cost.

Image: the character and qualities projected by a business.

Income: cash in return for business services or products.

Initial Balances: The amount of cash owned or debt owed by a business when an accounting system is begun.

Interest: the fee charged for or received from the use of money over time.

Invoice: a detailed listing of the services rendered, including an accounting of all costs, prepared by the person providing the service.

Letter of Agreement: a contract in letter form; an outline of the terms of the relationship; a confirmation of the arrangement between parties. (See also Agreement and Contract.)

Liability: an obligation to pay a debt (such as credit accounts, taxes, notes payable, or mortgage) to a creditor.

Licensing: the act of registering a business and obtaining the proper documents to operate legally; requirements differ by state and by industry.

Liquid: assets that are readily converted into cash.

Management: the process of planning, organizing, and controlling ones efforts, resources, and personnel to achieve vision, purpose, and goals and to earn income.

Market Research: the gathering and analyzing of data and facts to help make decisions for establishing and meeting marketing goals.

Marketing: promoting a product or service in the competitive environment to gain the greatest exposure while utilizing the least amount of resources—time, energy, money, and personnel.

Marketing Strategy: the overall process that will successfully promote a service or product and reach income objectives, implemented by: performing market research, creating a promotion plan and appropriate materials, and allocating and utilizing resources to carry out the plan.

Mentor: professional person, strong in certain business functions; chosen for support, advice, and empowerment.

Message Slant: the content and focus of the information in promotional materials intended to invoke a specific response from the reader.

Miscellaneous Summary: the summarizing of amounts in the Miscellaneous column of Receipts or Disbursements Journals into a total for each category.

Money Market Account: a savings account that yields a slightly higher interest rate, uses checks for withdrawals, and restricts the number of withdrawals permitted.

Net Loss: the amount by which expenses from a business exceed income.

Net Profit: the amount earned from business activities after all expenses have been deducted.

Net Worth: Owner's Investment + Assets - (Liabilities + Draw).

Networking: developing a matrix of individuals to share resources and skills for both personal gain and the greater good of all.

Note: money borrowed with a written promise to repay over a period of time, usually longer than one year.

Organizing: act of arranging and systematizing into an orderly, functional, structured, unified whole.

Outstanding Checks: checks that have not yet been paid by the bank during the statement period.

Overhead: the basic operating expenses of a business, including rent, utilities, telephone, postage, and so forth.

Partnership: a business owned and usually managed by two or more people, created by a written partnership agreement.

Payee: the person to whom payment is made.

Petty Cash: a nominal sum of money established as a separate cash fund from which cash disbursements are made for small expenses.

Planning: determining that which specifically needs to be done—when, how, by whom, and the necessary sequential order—to achieve management goals. Planning includes budgeting and time management, as well as program development and marketing strategies.

Positioning: establishing a business in the competitive environment of a service industry by taking and maintaining a solid place in the minds of target clients.

Positioning Message: the major features and benefits of the service, based on positioning objectives, which will become the focus of the campaign.

Positioning Objectives: positioning intention and goals, based in part on the growth stage of the service industry.

Positioning Slogan: a short phrase that specifically identifies the service and the desired position of a business in its service industry.

Preferred State: the desired, possible, but not necessarily current, situation or condition. (See also Current State.)

Problem Solving: a process in which one: 1) investigates the situation, defines the problem, identifies decision objectives, diagnoses the causes; 2) develops alternatives; 3) evaluates alternatives and selects the best one; and 4) implements and follows up the decision.

Profit and Loss Statement: a statement providing information about income and expenses over a specified period of time. Also known as Income Statement.

Profitability: ability of a business or program to create profit.

Program: the income-producing methodology and structure of the projects through which the service is provided.

Promotion: the process through which information is communicated to sell or popularize a service.

Promotion Plan: the step-by-step plan of promotional campaigns designed to promote success by increasing exposure, client base, and income.

Promotional Campaigns: the various methods and activities available to promote a business or service (e.g., advertising, direct sales, etc.).

Promotional Materials: cover letters, proposals, business cards, brochures, flyers, and other materials used for promotional purposes.

Promotional Strategy: the means for achieving goals outlined in the promotion plan, consisting of the objectives and message of a promotion, and based on the vision, purpose, goals, target clientele, and the growth stage of the service industry.

Psychographics: lifestyle characteristics of a certain population, determined for marketing purposes. (See also Demographics.)

Public Relations: the methods and activities of a business to expose it, present its services, and develop and maintain a favorable relationship with the public.

Publicity: information about a product, service, person, group, or event that is disseminated without charge by the media to attract public attention.

Quality: level of artistry and excellence.

Receipts Journal: the bookkeeping journal in which all inflows of cash are recorded, as listed on the Chart of Accounts.

Receipts Summary: the bookkeeping journal that records monthly and quarterly totals of income, from which financial statement figures are recorded.

Reflective Visioning: a meditative process, including a question format that facilitates reflection and evaluation of an issue in order to enhance clarity and facilitate decision making.

Refund: the reimbursement of a client's payment. A refund is a reduction in income—not an expense—recorded in the Disbursements Journal. It is correctly placed on the Profit and Loss Statement as a reduction in income. (See also Profit and Loss Statement.)

Reimbursement: the refund from a supplier for goods returned. It is not income, but is recorded in the Receipts Journal, then is placed on the Profit and Loss Statement as a reduction of the appropriate expense.

Resistance: a strong feeling that seems to be against an idea, suggestion, or action.

Resource: something that can be drawn upon and used for support: time, energy, personal strengths, other people, assets, capital, business skills, colleagues, networks.

Retainer: prepayment for services to be rendered by a professional, usually within a specified period of time.

Reversal: in a bookkeeping system, the subtraction of an entry previously made.

Re-visioning: the process of re-evaluating circumstances when they no longer fulfill personal needs and desires.

Sales: the process of creating a relationship to determine whether a service or product appropriately satisfies a need or desire.

Sales Promotion: a periodic, one-time sales effort and/or demonstration.

Schedule C: the tax form used by sole proprietors or partners, called "Profit (or Loss) from Business or Profession."

Self-management: the process of managing one's energy, activities, and resources in order to give form to the vision.

Service: the intention to provide benefit through vital action; that which you "do" for your client.

Service Charge: a charge added to a client's regular fee for late or extended payments, returned checks, or any other irregular circumstances, such as a rush charge. Also, a bank charge for items such as returned checks, charge card payment processing, etc.

Service Industry: the specific segment of commerce in which your business is categorized.

Service Industry's Growth Stage: the stage of development of a service industry (e.g., infancy, growth, shakeout, maturity, late maturity).

Shadow: an inner quality, aspect, or function that, although denied and hidden, nevertheless has a strong effect on the character and condition of one's life.

Short-term Loan: money borrowed for less than one year.

Social Need: a need held by a segment of society or by society in general (e.g., food, shelter, medical care, education) that can be satisfied by business.

Sole Proprietorship: an unincorporated business owned and usually managed by one person.

Solvency: ability of a business to meet its financial obligations.

Source Document: invoice or sales receipt that supplies information about a transaction.

Start-up Budget: a determination of the amount of money needed to begin a business and operate it for an initial, specified period of time.

Start-up Capital: the initial money needed to begin a business.

Success: the achievement of something envisioned, desired, or needed, as personally defined.

Support: to aid, advocate, or lend strength to.

Target Clientele: the specific clientele, as determined by demographic and psychographic evaluation, for whom a marketing strategy is designed.

Time Management: organizing activities to make the best use of the time available.

Typesetter: a person who sets type for printed materials.

Variance Statement: an accounting statement that compares actual expenses and income with amounts projected in the budget.

Venture Capital: equity financing raised from private investors who are represented by an investment banker or venture capital firm.

Vision: the picture of the preferred life imagined from one's yearnings, desires, and needs; an idea that inspires one to create life at a high level of quality.

Visioning: 1) visualizing the preferred state or future situation that will satisfy needs and wants so that, with planning, the vision functions at the most supportive level for all concerned; 2) using this process to recognize and overcome inertia and limitations and to create needed changes.

◆

"Now is the only time there is."
Brian Malloy

Appendix B.

Business Proposal

If you do not have the money needed to adequeately capitalize your business, you will need to borrow it from others. To do so, show that you know what you are doing and how you will do it: describe your service, how much money you will generate from it, how you will use the money, and how and when you will repay it. In addition, be clear about what you plan to do for the next five years.

Your business proposal translates your vision, goals, and strategy into a description of decisions and actions. It explains how you intend to fulfill these, with costs, income projections, profit, and required capitalization. It includes documentation of financial history and presents projections for your financial future. The proposal should also include a résumé of work experience and education, as well as reference letters.

This proposal is a simplified version of a business plan. It is created as you complete the written activities in this manual. Keep it current, making changes when your vision, purpose and function change, or as life circumstances alter. When you keep your plan current, you become aligned with the events in the world around you. In the process, you will decide and act from intelligent evaluation and thus know you are doing your best.

Here are some suggestions for keeping your business plan up-to-date:

- Review your plan every few weeks, at first, and revise it to reflect changes. As your stability and confidence increase and your direction feels solid, regular six-month reviews will be adequate.

- Every six months or so, redo the visioning process (Current Vision, Activity 2), as well as any other activities that will help you with your business.

- Create a file for articles, reports, and other information related to your business and service industry.

- Make a file for projects you want to do in the future.

To capitalize your new or existing business, you have four sources of capital:

- Your own savings and assets
- Friends, family, colleagues
- Banks
- Private lenders

These sources are listed in the order we suggest you follow to raise money. Begin by evaluating your own resources first: savings, IRA, stocks, items of value, including your car, equipment, or house. If you don't have excess resources, you can raise money from any of the other three catagories you choose.

It is usually easier to borrow money from those who care about you and want to see you succeed—family, friends, close colleagues. Without a solid plan, track record, and financial statements, you won't be able to demonstrate to lenders that you are viable and safe.

Banks offer debt financing and secure it with your collateral. If you are an individual in a service business, your financial needs are probably modest. If your business needs are more complicated, and require larger amounts of money, refer to other books and resources for information on other methods of raising money.

Regardless of whom you approach for capitalization, you need a proposal. This should be a simple, straightforward explanation of your business, goals, and needs. A proposal for your service business, with projected income, expenses, and profits for the next one to five years, will be from six to ten pages in length, plus supporting documentation and letters. If you have several programs or a complex one, your proposal will be longer. Be prepared to present a potential lender with additional information as requested.

Lenders often require collateral—something of yours you sign over to them that they can sell if you don't repay them. If you are buying valuable equipment with a high resale value, you will be considered less of a risk, which will help secure your financing. Your car, savings, IRA, stocks, saleable equipment, and house are potential collateral. You may be required to put up collateral that is valued in excess of the amount you borrow.

Lenders want a proposal that answers these questions:

- What are your purpose, business, and goals?
- How will you fulfill these?
- How much money will you need?
- How are you going to repay it?
- What collateral will you put up to secure financing?
- How will you repay it if your initial plan fails?

Business Proposal Outline

The outline that follows is comprehensive. If your business is simple, you may not want to include every detail indicated. Read it carefully, and use your discretion.

1. **Introduction.** This is a one-page sketch that explains your service, goals, and plan, and should make the reader want to know more. Though it begins your proposal, you may find it easier to write it last. It should include the following:

a. A one-sentence mission statement describing your service, followed by a paragraph explaining how the service will operate.

b. A paragraph describing your income-generating programs.

c. A brief profile of your typical clients.

d. A paragraph about your major competitors.

e. A description of your service's unique contribution. Include discussion of the market's need for your service.

f. The amount of capital you need, and a paragraph summarizing your five-year plan.

2. **Business Description.** This section describes your business in detail, emphasizing your strengths and accomplishments. If you haven't yet been in this business, include your résumé of work experience, expertise, and professional accomplishments.

   The rest of your plan should expand your introductory statement into full descriptions and explanations.

   a. Nature of your business: what you do, and why.

   b. Business history: when and how your present business evolved; its legal structure.

   c. Service: your service and income-producing program; any contracts in place or under negotiation.

   d. Client profile: who is ready for your service and why.

   e. Service industry: the social need your industry satisfies, its growth stage, and trends.

   f. Competition: describe your major competitors and compare price, size of business, share of market each holds, and the apparent financial strength of each.

   g. Promotion plan: describe the mix of promotional campaigns you will use to reach your clients and the income you project.

   h. Future: describe future programs and projected revision of your present service and plans; include your one-and five-year plans.

3. **Management.** Lenders know that planning and effective management are key to your success. Put careful thought into your proposal to show them that you are a safe risk. You can add to your management strength by including your accountant, lawyer, mentors, and select adjunct consultants.

a. Describe yourself and other owners or personnel. Include information about their backgrounds, achievements, skills and strengths, and describe how the business will be managed.

b. Include short descriptions of all adjunct consultants, such as bank, insurance, attorney, accountant, consultants, mentors, etc..

c. If your request includes money for future personnel or consultants, indicate what they will do, how, and when they will begin.

4. **Proposed Financing.** Be specific about the amount of money you request, and what you will do with it. Include:

   a. Exactly the amount you need and when.

   b. Specifically how you will use the loan proceeds, and when.

   c. Include a budget of your financial income and expense projections.

   d. A proposed schedule for repaying the debt. This should be realistic, by aligning repayment with increased income.

   e. A statement of the personal assets you will pledge as collateral, if any, and whether you will sign a guarantee.

5. **Risk Factors.** Explain the risks of doing this business, and how you will address them. Remember that risks always exist, and by addressing them openly, you show that you are aware, realistic and prepared.

6. **Financial Data.** Include your complete past financial statements, if you have been in business. If you have not been in business, include statements of your income history. (Your accountant can help you prepare these.)

7. **Support Documentation.** Résumé of work experience, emphasizing your experience related to this business; and reference letters from high-profile people familiar with your skills, expertise and credibility.

◆

Appendix C.

Resources for Starting a Business

When you begin organizing your business, you will find that there are numerous activities to do, many of which you identified in Activity 4, Business Evaluation; Activity 5, Organizing Your Business; and Activity 11, Program Planning and Development. The following resources will help you identify and satisfy other necessary activities, as well as provide you with additional information.

1. **Chamber of Commerce.** Your local Chamber should be your first stop. They can often save you time by providing you with local regulations and relevant book lists and checklists.

   In many communities, the Chamber may provide Small Business Administration pamphlets and services. They also have programs to help introduce new businesses into the community and to provide networking opportunities, especially for smaller businesses. And finally, the Chamber may be able to provide you with market research information about your community.

2. **Local Public Education.** The business school of your local university, college, or the Continuing Education program of a local college may have a small business assistance center.

3. **Licensing Requirements.** Every state and local municipality has its own requirements for registering businesses. To be sure your service business complies, contact your state, county, and city governments to determine the proper licensing authority and which regulations apply.

   a. State:

      1) The Department of Regulatory Agencies issues licenses for specific professions. In some states, this agency may have a Start a Business Kit that includes all state and some federal forms. If not, ask if another department has such a kit.

      2) The Revenue Department provides sales and other tax information. Some states require trade name registration through the Revenue Department. In others, it is done at the local level.

      3) If you are incorporating, file incorporation papers with the Secretary of State.

   b. County:

      1) Contact the county Revenue Department for sales tax information.

Empowering Vision

      2) If you live outside the city limits, contact the county Planning Department regarding zoning restrictions.

      3) If you are opening a food service or performing a service that might impact the general health, water or air supply, contact your local Health Department.

  c. City:

      1) Check with the city Planning Office for zoning regulations.

      2) Check with the city Clerk about registering your trade name and for city sales and personal property tax information. Also ask if there are any other taxes for which you may be liable.

4. **Credit Cards.** If you wish to accept credit cards in payment for your services or products, determine how much it will cost you to do so.

  a. Begin by calling the bank where you have a checking account, then call around to several other banks in your area to see if their fees vary.

  Ask each bank the following questions:

      1) What is the application fee, if any, and what percentage of sales will they retain for their fee? (MasterCard/Visa are usually about 3-4 percent, depending on the volume). Are any other fees involved?

      2) Will you need to purchase an imprinter (about $20) or is it provided?

      3) Are the required sales forms and credit slips free?

      4) Will they provide credit card logos you can use in your advertising?

      5) Can you offer MasterCard and Visa with one application and use the same forms?

  b. Call American Express, Discover, Diner's Club, and other companies to learn about their requirements and fees. Determine if your target clientele uses these cards before applying to accept them.

5. **Insurance and Bonding.** You will probably need business liability insurance, especially if you are engaged in a service that could endanger your clients or their personal property. Talk to several agencies for types and costs of insurance. Bonding services insure that your clients' money and their personal possessions are safe while they are with you. To learn more about these services, look in the Yellow Pages under Bonding Services or Bonds—Surety and Fidelity. Often these are the same firms that offer business and liability insurance.

6. **Collections.** Help support your clients in staying current with their payments to you. If needed, collection agencies often keep half of what they collect. Of course, half is more than

nothing. Many states have bad check laws that protect businesses and make it profitable to pursue even small amounts. Talk to several collection agencies to find one you are comfortable working with. Also, contact the Small Claims Court (city or county) to learn about their procedures. Also refer to Exercise 13, Fees, Discounts, and Collections.

7. **Community Resources.**

    a. Local Chambers of Commerce. These organizations offer seminars and networking opportunities. They may also have SCORE (Service Corps of Retired Executives) counseling, which provides free advice for new or small businesses.

    b. Local business organizations. These include business and service organizations such as Rotary International and Kiwanis for men, and Zonta and Business and Professional Women (BPW) for women. Research your community to see if there is a Win/Win Business Forum. (See f3 below.)

    c. Public Library. A great source of information—reference librarians are particularly helpful.

        1) Look for the *Encyclopedia of Associations*. If there is a professional association for your industry, it will be listed, along with addresses, publications, dues, etc. This book can also give you marketing ideas. The *Directory of Directories* is a similar treasure of information.

        2) Ask the reference librarian if the library subscribes to *Standard Rate and Data Service*. These directories list advertising rates for major magazines, newspapers, and trade journals. Again, these are helpful for market research.

        3) Your library can provide local census and other demographic data.

    d. University Libraries. A business school library provides many additional resources for market research, giving you access to many management journals and trade magazines that are not available in municipal libraries. Librarians are very helpful and may also assist with computer database searches.

    e. Yellow Pages. Great for discovering your competition, looking for clients, and general good reading!

    f. Local Newspaper and Weekly Community Publications.

        1) Read the ads and the sections your clients read for marketing ideas and leads.

        2) Read the help wanted ads. They will tell you which industries and companies are hiring (therefore expanding). Propose working as a consultant to save a company payroll costs.

        3) Read the calendar sections to find service and networking clubs, or opportuni-

Empowering Vision

ties for giving talks or volunteering your services to enhance your business. (See 7b above.)

8. **National Resources.**

   a. Small Business Association (SBA).

   1) Check the telephone directory under "U.S. Government" for the nearest SBA office. Ask for a list of free Management Assistance Publications.

   2) Call the Answer Desk Hotline, 1-800-827-5722 (in Washington, DC, 202-653-7561) Monday through Friday, 9 a.m. to 5 p.m. Eastern time, with questions about government agencies that provide assistance to businesses, Small Business Innovation Research (SBIR) grants, and venture capital funding. They can also give you information about copyrights, franchises, licenses, publications, taxes, etc.

   b. Patent and Trademark Office (703) 557-7800, U.S. Department of Commerce, Washington, DC 20231. Request copies of *General Information Concerning Trademarks, Questions and Answers About Patents, General Information Concerning Patents,* and *Patents and Inventions: An Information Aid for Inventors.*

   c. Copyright Information, Register Copyrights, Library of Congress, Washington, DC 20540. Request *General Information on Copyrights.*

   d. Internal Revenue Service. Call your local office and request *Tax Guide for Small Businesses, Tax Withholding and Declaration of Estimated Tax, Information on Self-Employment Tax,* and *Use of Home Office,* as appropriate. (See Taxes, Page 159.)

   e. Minority Business Development Agency, Department of Commerce, Room 6708, Washington, DC 20203, 202-377-1936, publishes *Minority Business Today,* a bimonthly newsletter covering assistance and government contracts for minority-owned businesses.

   f. National Economic Development Association, 1730 M Street NW, Washington, DC 20036, provides free financial and technical assistance, help in obtaining loans, business and management seminars, assistance in securing government and private contracts.

   g. Small Business Innovation Research (SBIR). Program grants are available for research in various areas through several government agencies. Write SBIR, Office of Innovation, Research and Technology, 409 3rd Street SW, Washington, DC 20416. (202) 205-6450.

◆

Bibliography

Albert, Tessa Warschaw, Ph.D. *Rich is Better: How women can bridge the gap between wanting and having it all: financially, emotionally, professionally* (Doubleday, 1987).

Atkinson, William. *Working at Home: Is It for You?* (Dow Jones-Irwin, 1985).

Auer, J.T. *Joy of Selling: A Book of Ideas, Opportunities and Renewal* (Longman Trade, 1989).

Beecher, Willard and Marguerite. *Beyond Success and Failure* (Dallas, TX: Willard and Marguerite Beecher Foundation, 1966).

Bry, Adelaide. *Visualization - Directing the Movies of Your Mind* (New York: B&N, 1979).

Burka, Jane B., Ph.D. and Lenora M. Yuen, Ph.D. *Procrastination: Why You Do It, What to Do About It* (Reading, MA: Addison-Wesley, 1983).

Butterworth, Eric. *Spiritual Economics* (Unity School of Christianity, 1983).

Catalyst Group Staff. *Marketing Yourself* (Bantam, 1981).

Clason, George S. *The Richest Man in Babylon* (Bantam Books, 1985).

Davidson, Jeffrey P. *Marketing on a Shoestring: Low-Cost Tips for Marketing Your Products or Services* (Wiley, 1988).

Dible, Donald M. *Up Your OWN Organization! A Handbook on How to Start and Finance a New Business* (Reston, VA: Reston Publishing, 1974). Contains an exhaustive list of recommended reading.

Drucker, Peter F. *Innovation and Entrepreuneurship: Practice and Principles* (Harper-Row, 1985)

Fisher, Roger and Ury, William. *Getting to Yes: Negotiating Agreement Without Giving In* (Penguin, 1983).

Foundation for Inner Peace. *A Course in Miracles* (Tiburon, CA: Foundation for Inner Peace, 1976).

Friedman, Milton and Friedman, Rose. *Free to choose: A Personal Statement* (Harcourt Brace Jovanovich, 1991).

Fritz, Robert. *The Path of Least Resistance* (Salem, MA: Stillpoint Publishing Co., 1970).

Fritz, Robert. *A Short Course in Creating What You Always Wanted to But Couldn't Before Because Nobody Ever Told You How Because They Didn't Know Either* (Salem, MA: DMA, Inc.).

Gawain, Shakti. *Creative Visualization* (San Rafael, CA: Whatever Publishing, 1978).

Gawain, Shakti. *Living in the Light* (San Rafael, CA: Whatever Publishing, 1986).

Gerber, Michael E. *E-Myth: Why Most Businesses Don't Work and What to do About It* (Ballinger Publishing, 1985).

Gumpert, David E., editor. *Growing Concerns: Building and Managing the Smaller Business* (New York: John Wiley & Sons, 1984). Part of the Harvard Business Review Executive Book Series.

Guaspari, John. *Customer Connection: Quality for the Rest of Us* (AMACOM, 1988).

Harmon, Willis, Ph.D. and Howard Rheingold. *Higher Creativity* (Los Angeles: J. P. Tarcher, 1984).

Hawken, Paul. *Growing a Business* (Simon & Schuster, 1987).

Hawken, Paul. *The Next Economy* (Ballantine, 1984).

Holtz, Herman. *How to Succeed as an Independent Consultant* (New York: John Wiley & Sons, 1983).

Houston, Jean. *The Possible Human: A Course in Extending Your Physical, Mental and Creative Abilities* (Los Angeles, J.P. Tarcher, 1982).

Hubbard, Barbara Marx. *Evolutionary Journey: A Personal Guide to a Positive Future* (Berkeley, CA: Mindbody, 1985).

Jampolsky, Gerald, G., M.D. *Love Is Letting Go of Fear* (New York: Bantam, 1982).

Johnson, Spencer and Larry Wilson. *The One Minute Salesperson* (New York: Morrow, 1984).

Kamoroff, Bernard, CPA. *Small-Time Operator: How to Start Your Own Small Business, Keep Your Books, Pay Your Taxes, and Stay Out of Trouble!* (Laytonville, CA: Bell Springs, 1981).

Laborde, Genie Z. *Influencing With Integrity* (Palo Alto, CA: Syntony Publishing, 1987).

Lakein, Alan. *How to get Control of your Time and your Life* (New York: Signet, 1973).

Lant, Jeffrey, Ph.D. T*he Unabashed Self-Promoter's Guide: What every man, woman, child, and oragnization in America needs to know about getting ahead by exploiting the Media* (Cambridge: JLA Publications, 1983).

Levinson, Jay Conrad. *Guerrilla Marketing: Secrets for Making Big Profits from Your Small Business* (Boston: Houghton Mifflin, 1984).

Levitt, Theodore. *The Marketing Imagination* (Free Press, 1983).

Milling, Bryan E. *Cash Flow Problem Solver* (Radnor, PA: Chilton Book Co., 1984).

Mouser, Ferdinand F. and David J. Schwartz. *American Business* (San Diego, CA: Harcourt, Brace, Jovanovich, 1986).

Ostrander, Sheila and Lynn Schroeder with Nancy Ostrander. *Super-Learning* (New York: Dell Publishing, 1979).

Patent, Arnold M. *You Can Have It All* (Piermont, NY: Money Mastery Publishing, 1984).

Peck, M. Scott, M.D. *The Road Less Travelled* (New York: Simon & Schuster, 1978).

Phillips, Michael and Salli Rasberry. *Marketing Without Advertising* (Berkeley, CA: Nold Press, 1986).

Ponder, Catherine. *The Dynamic Laws of Prosperity* (Marina del Rey, CA: DeVorss and Company, 1985).

Ray, Michael and Rochelle Myers. *Creativity in Business* (Garden City, NY: Doubleday & Co., 1986). **Based on the Stanford University course that has revolutionized the art of success.**

Rice, Craig S. *Marketing Without a Marketing Budget* (Beckman Publishing, 1989).

Ries, Al and Jack Trout. *Positioning: The Battle for Your Mind* (New York: Warner Books, 1981).

Robbins, Anthony. *Unlimited Power* (Fawcett, 1987).

Rowan, Roy. *The Intuitive Manager* (Boston: Little Brown and Company, 1986).

Russell, Peter. *The Global Brain* (Los Angeles, J.P. Tarcher, Inc., 1983).

Small Business Administration. *Starting and Managing a Small Business of Your Own.* Order from U.S. Government Printing Office, Washington, DC 20402.

Small, Jacquelyn. *Transformers* (Marina del Rey, CA: DeVorss and Company, 1982).

Van Kaspel, Venita. *The Power of Money Dynamics* (Reston, VA: Reston Publishing, 1983).

◆

Index

Accounting 17, 21, 51, 52, 117-124, 145
    Accrual basis 51, 118
    cash basis 51, 117, 119, 120, 122, 124
    period 128, 133, 146, 151
Accounts
    Payable 118
    Receivable 51, 52, 118
Advertising 87-92, 100, 123, 140, 152, 161
Agreements (also see Contracts) 56-57
Assets 117, 120-122, 124, 125, 133, 140, 144, 155-157, 181, 184

Balance Sheet 121, 122, 138, 144-146, 155, 158
Bank
    charges 123, 140, 142, 146, 170, 171
    credits 136, 169, 171
    debits 169, 171
    statement 17, 121, 168-170
    reconciliation 144, 168,
Benefit(s) 34, 40, 63, 71, 84, 85, 98, 102, 109, 111, 113
Bonding 13, 186
Bookkeeping 16, 20, 117-119, 121, 169
Break-even Calculation 94, 161-164
    analysis 42,
Brochure 81, 84, 100, 111-113
Budget 23, 42, 100, 111, 113, 121, 127, 130, 140, 150-154, 162, 184
    operating 15, 22, 23
    start-up 15, 22
Business
    cards 81, 84, 100, 111, 114-115
    Evaluation and Checklist 13-17
    functions 21, 22, 26, 32, 60
    image 40
    letterhead 81, 84, 100, 111, 112
    location 17, 35
    naming your 82
    organization 1, 19-23, 32, 59
    Proposal 17, 181-184

Campaigns, promotional 65-66, 80-81, 86, 100
Capital, start-up 15, 17, 21, 181-184
Cash
    basis accounting 117-118, 124,
    flow 44, 47, 52, 100, 127, 130, 133, 161
    In Bank 122, 124, 133, 156
Chart of Accounts 17, 122-124, 125, 128-130, 140
Checking account 124, 144, 155, 168-171
Certified Public Accountant (CPA) 16, 117-120

Client(s)
    profile 15, 65, 67-69, 84, 183
    Prospective Client Profile 103-104
    service area 73, 76-78, 85, 87, 89, 93
    state 40, 112
    targeting your ideal 67-68
Cold calls 16, 106-107
Collateral 182, 184
Collections 15, 50, 52-54, 187
Competition 15, 63, 65-66, 70-73, 77, 93, 133
Complimentary services 94, 95, 99
Computer bulletin boards 89
Contract(s) 15, 56-58, 61, 183
Corporation 14, 118-120, 159, 185
Cost(s) (see Expenses)
Cover letter 16, 100, 109-110
CPA (see Certified Public Accountant)
CPM (see Critical Path Method)
Critical Path Method (CPM) 22, 24-28, 32, 66, 100

Debt (see Liabilities)
Demographics 67, 87, 90, 94, 187
Department of Revenue 14, 159, 185
Depreciation 124, 146, 148
Direct mail 89, 122
Direct sales 16, 86, 92-94, 98, 103-104, 106-107
Disbursements
    cash 17, 121, 165
    Journal 17, 121, 133, 135-136, 140-144, 146, 165, 169
    miscellaneous 142
    Summary 121, 142, 144-146, 155
Discount Schedule 52, 136
Discount(s) 50-52, 92, 95, 123, 136
    certificate 93
Draw 123, 125, 135, 140, 155-156

Equity 123-125, 155-156
Expense(s) 42-43, 55, 118, 121-125, 129, 135-136, 140, 142, 144-146, 150-151, 161
    cost(s) 22, 122, 124, 127-128, 161, 181
    fixed 127, 161-164
    miscellaneous 123, 129, 142
    overhead 23, 42, 127, 161-162
    petty cash 165
    program 23, 42, 124, 127, 162
    projections 129, 182, 184
    start-up 15, 22
    variable 127, 161-162, 164

Fee(s) 14, 41, 42, 46, 50-52, 68, 130, 161-163, 187
Filing system 15, 23, 59-61
Financial
    loss 123, 125, 130, 145-146, 151, 155-156,
        161, 177
    management 1, 118
    map 122
    period 118, 127, 128, 146, 151
    profit 42, 117, 118, 123-125, 130, 145, 146-147,
        155-157, 159, 161, 181, 182
    statements 17, 43, 120, 130, 145-158, 182, 184
Flyers 81, 89, 100, 111, 112
Fixed expenses (see Expenses, fixed)
Free Publications 87

Gift Certificates 94, 99, 100
Growth Stage(s) (see Service industry growth stages)
Graphics 111, 124

Image 14, 34-36, 68, 71, 81, 82, 85, 90, 92, 114-115
Income 14, 22, 37, 42, 45, 52, 68, 94, 99, 118, 120-122,
    125, 128, 145-152, 155, 161-163
    net 145-146, 156
    generating program 14, 21-25, 34, 37, 39, 41, 45,
        65, 127-128
    projections 46, 127, 129, 130, 181-184
    sources of 133, 146
Industry 12, 44, 46, 66, 70, 87, 93, 112
Incorporating (see Corporation)
Infancy stage 73, 76-77
Interest 52, 123, 125, 133-135, 136, 147, 159, 169-171
Insurance 13, 17, 21, 57, 123, 184, 186
Internal Revenue Service (IRS) 54-55, 59, 119,
    159, 188
Invoice 15, 52-55, 61, 118

Late maturity stage 73, 74, 79
Lawyer 17, 119, 184
Leads
    from client 92
    from competitors 64, 92
    potential 92, 97, 187
Leasehold improvements 140, 155-156
Legal structures 119-120, 183
Lenders 181-183
Letter
    cover 109-110
    of Agreement 56-57
Liabilities 117, 121-123, 125, 144, 155, 156
    debt 117, 119-120, 124, 155, 184
Licensing 16, 21, 119, 185
Limited Liability Company 119-120
Loan(s)
    long-term (see Notes)
    short-term 125, 155-156

Magazines 87, 90, 95-96, 187
Mailing list 95, 104, 107

Management 25
    business 1, 10-11, 21
    financial 117-118, 120-121, 125, 127, 150, 168
    time 24-33, 66
Marketing 11, 21, 25, 63-67, 86, 92, 99, 187
    budget 65
    strategy 37, 44, 63-66, 73, 161
Market research 15, 63-66, 71, 79, 185, 187
Master list 20-21, 40, 41
Master Schedule (see Time Management)
Maturity stage 74, 78
Money
    Market Account 122, 124-125, 133, 140, 155-156
    raising for business 181-184

Naming your business 13, 82-83
Narrowcasting 88
Narrowing Your Focus 22, 37-38,
Net Worth 117, 121-123, 125, 144, 145, 155, 156
Networking 16, 29, 65, 95-98, 100, 185, 187, 188
Newsletters 88, 96, 112
Newspapers 64, 70, 71, 87, 93, 96, 187
Note(s) 157
    long-term 123, 125, 155, 156
    payable 123

Objections, handling of 104
Objective(s), promotional 80, 82
Organization 1, 21, 32, 40, 59
Organizational Structures 118-120
    types of 119-120

Partnership 14, 119-120, 159
Patents and Trademarks 188
Payment(s) 50, 52-55, 133, 187
    late/overdue 135
Petty Cash 17, 123, 124, 135, 144, 156, 165-167
Planning 1, 7, 11, 19-24, 26, 29
    Chart (see Time Management)
    promotional materials 81, 111-115

Policy(ies) 15, 50, 52-58
Positioning 80-85
    message/slant 65, 80, 81, 84, 85, 99, 107,
        111, 113
    objectives 16, 65, 80-82, 98, 99, 107, 112
    slogan 65, 81, 83-84, 112,
Posters 89, 100
Presentation, Sales 16, 92, 103, 104
Press release 95
Product planning 39
Professional associations/groups 97, 187
Profit and Loss Statement 17, 121, 125, 130, 135, 136,
    138, 142, 144-147, 150, 151-156
Program
    budget 42, 100
    development 19, 21, 25, 41
    expenses 42, 127, 162

implementation 19, 21, 25, 41
management 40-41
organization 21, 40-41
outline 40, 111
Planning & Development 22, 25, 29, 39, 43, 60, 65, 129, 162
requirements 40-42
research and design 20
viability 41, 42, 161-164
Projection(s)
    budget 127, 129, 150
    financial 146, 163
Promotion(al) 16, 21, 44, 84-86, 89, 98, 112
    campaigns 65-66, 80-81, 86, 183
    costs and expenses 42, 124, 140, 146, 154
    materials 16, 35, 63, 65, 71, 81, 84, 100, 111-115
    message 81, 84-85, 111, 113
    plan 16, 64-66, 86, 100, 183
    sales 86, 93-95, 100
    themes 99
Psychographics 67-68, 90, 94
Public Relations 19, 21, 25, 28, 86, 95-97
    campaign 95
Publicity 16, 65, 89, 95, 96

Radio
    advertising 87-88
    talk shows 96
Receipts
    cash 17, 121, 133
    Journal 17, 52, 94, 121, 133, 139
    Miscellaneous 136
    Summary 121, 136, 145, 146
Refund(s) 123, 133, 136, 142, 144, 146
Reimbursement 135-136
Reversing an entry 135

SBA (see Small Business Administration)
SCORE (Senior Corp. of Retired Execs.) 51, 187
S Corporation 119, 120
Sales 16, 66, 93, 96, 97, 101-103, 106
    cold calls 106, 107
    commissions 93, 100, 124
    Direct 92, 106-107
    follow-up 104, 107
    phone calls 104, 106, 107
    Presentation 16, 80, 81, 92, 96, 103, 104
    Process 102, 103, 104
    Promotions 86, 93-95
    warm calls 106
Savings account 122, 124, 125, 133, 140, 155,
Schedule C 119, 125, 144, 159
Schedule SE 119, 159
Scheduling 25, 27
Seasonal flows 44-45, 129
Self, Evaluation 10-12
    management 1, 2
Service
    charges 53, 54, 57, 58, 125, 133, 135, 169,
    complimentary 94, 95, 99

industry 15, 16, 45, 50, 63, 64, 71-79, 83, 84, 181, 183
    industry growth stages 15, 65, 73-79, 179, 183
Shakeout stage 74, 77-78
Sheet, Balance 121, 122, 138, 144-146, 155-157
Short-term loan 123, 125, 155, 156
Slogan 16, 65, 83, 85
Small Business Association (SBA) 51, 185, 188
Social Security 159
Sole proprietor (ship) 10, 14, 118-119, 159
Standard Rate & Data Service (SRDS) 87, 89

Targeting clients 67
Tax(es) 17, 55, 117, 129, 136, 144, 159, 185-186, 188
    estimated 129, 159
Television 87, 88
    advertising 88
    talk shows 96
Time Management 1, 22, 24-33, 66
    CPM (see Critical Path Method)
    Master Schedule 27, 29, 30, 99
    Planning Chart 22, 27, 32-34, 41
Trade Name 14, 185, 186
Trade Journals 64, 87, 93, 95, 98, 187

Variable expenses (see Expenses, variable)
Variance Statement 17, 121, 130, 145, 150-154
Vision 2-9, 14, 121
    Current 3, 7, 8, 22, 38
    Life-Purpose 3, 4, 7, 38
Visioning 1-9, 22

Workload 14, 22, 43-46, 99, 101, 117

Yellow Pages 64, 70, 71, 76, 89, 92, 187
Your Service, Quality, & Image 34-35, 37, 65, 111

Zoning requirements 17, 186

TO ORDER BOOKS AND RECEIVE INFORMATION

To order copies of *Empowering Vision:* *(please print)*

Name _____

Address _____

City/State/Zip _____ Phone _____

Shipping Address *(if different)* _____

City/State/Zip _____

Please send me _____ copies at $17.95 each.
(2-4 for $14.35 each)

Subtotal

Shipping/handling: $3.00 first book
$1.50 each additional book

Colorado residents only
include 6% sales tax

Total Amount

Send your order, along with your check or money order to:

*a*imari Press
P.O. Box 18296
Boulder, CO 80303-8296
(303) 442-0681
Phone orders: 1-800-285-3653

For wholesale and larger quantity discounts, call (303) 442-0681.

Please send information on the following:

- ☐ Planning an *Empowering Vision* workshop in your area.
- ☐ Training programs for your small business and/or sales staff.
- ☐ Consultations with Marianne Weidlein.
- ☐ Other books and tapes by Marianne Weidlein.

Name _____

Address _____

City/State/Zip _____ Phone _____

Best times to call _____